What people are saying about . . .

Worshiping God in Spirit and in Truth

"*Worshiping God in Spirit and in Truth* is a book that will enlighten your understanding as to what God desires, but also inspire your heart to live a life filled with praise."

Pastor Jim Cymbala
The Brooklyn Tabernacle

"In *Worshiping God in Spirit and in Truth*, we are reminded that worship is not a show put on by an entertaining band on a Sunday morning. It is about establishing a genuine connection with the only One who deserves our praise. Almighty God, shake us and stir us, as we allow You to shift us from the status quo, and let this generation truly worship You in spirit and in truth."

Pastor Eddie Luke
Sanderson Christian Revival Center

"In her first book, *When You're in the Sunset, There's Sunshine Awaiting You*, Jennifer pointed us to Jesus. That is all that this life is meant to be—taking every opportunity to share the Gospel and to worship Him. Now, in her second book, she continues to give every ounce of praise to Christ!"

Evie Tornquist Karlsson
Evie Music

"A refreshing look at what worship truly is from a sweet spirited believer who knows what it means to worship the Lord in spirit and truth. Jennifer understands what it means to give all of the glory to the One who is most deserving of all praise. I encourage you to read it with an open heart and mind and allow the Lord to speak to you about true worship. Thank you, Jennifer, for your insights."

Pastor David McKeithen
Antioch Baptist Church

"Jennifer and I became friends when my husband and I were serving the church she attends. She has a very strong faith, which is so evident in her words, actions, and warm smile. She truly is God's disciple through her written words and the music she writes and performs to worship and honor God. I found her first book to be inspiring, and I am sure this book will touch your heart and mind to bring Jesus closer to you so that you will want to worship Him in a more meaningful way."

Janet Parker

Worshiping God

in Spirit and in Truth

Worshiping God

in Spirit and in Truth

Jennifer Campbell

Foreword by Ken Campbell

Cover Photography: Ken Campbell

Photo Location: Prince Christian Sound, Greenland

Cover and Interior Design: Jennifer Campbell

Library of Congress Control Number: 2020920583

ISBN: 978-0-9600359-2-2 (softcover)
ISBN: 978-0-9600359-3-9 (eBook)

Printed in the United States of America

To Jesus Christ

You are the Author and Finisher of my faith. You have loved me unconditionally since before I was even born. Without You, I would not be alive today. I love You with all of my heart and all of my soul. I shall worship and adore You forevermore, my Savior and my Lord.

"But the time is coming—indeed it's here now—when true worshipers will worship the Father in spirit and in truth. The Father is looking for those who will worship him that way. For God is Spirit, so those who worship him must worship in spirit and in truth."

—*John 4:23-24*

Contents

Contents

Contents

Foreword

"But the hour cometh, and now is, when the true worshippers shall worship the Father in spirit and in truth: for the Father seeketh such to worship him. God is a Spirit: and they that worship him must worship him in spirit and in truth" (John 4:23-24 KJV).

*W*hat does it mean to worship the Father in spirit and in truth? Does it mean to sit in an auditorium as a spectator for an hour or so each week? Does it mean practicing some complicated ceremonies or rituals? Does it mean focusing intently on a religious relic or icon? Does it mean listening to or singing songs that have little connection to your secular life? Throughout the week, are you, "Speaking to yourselves in psalms and hymns and spiritual songs, singing and making melody in your heart to the Lord" (Eph. 5:19 KJV), or are you programming your soul with the secular tunes of the Siren song? Real spiritual life with the Father is inseparable from secular life. Anything less is not spiritual life, but spiritual death. Watching a weekly performance or ritual is not true worship. True worship of our Heavenly Father must be the central focus of our lives, not a religious accessory. The true and living God will not be an ornament or decoration in your life.

Of course, idols have nothing to do with worshiping the Father in spirit and in truth. The same can be said for various "Christian" idols, icons, relics, bone fragments, and other items. God says, "You must not bow down to them or worship them, for I, the LORD your God, am a jealous God who will not tolerate your affection for any other gods" (Exod. 20:5). If you are venerating or bowing down to any material objects, even if you find them in a church building, remember, "God is a Spirit: and they that worship him must worship him in spirit and in truth" (John 4:24 KJV).

Several years ago, a religious leader in Eastern Europe told me he absolutely did not worship icons. He said that was a common misunderstanding of his religious tradition. Yet, a few minutes later, he spoke of praying to certain powerful icons to receive healing and blessings of various kinds. Nevertheless, no icon has any power whatsoever. The dead characteristics of idols are discussed in five different locations in the Bible. The last reference is in the book of Revelation, and it describes people who have suffered greatly, but still refuse to repent and worship the true and living God: "And the rest of the men which were not killed by these plagues yet repented not of the works of their hands, that they should not worship devils, and idols of gold, and silver, and brass, and stone, and of wood: which neither can see, nor hear, nor walk: Neither repented they of their murders, nor of their sorceries [including drugs, *pharmakeia* in the original Greek], nor of their fornication, nor of their thefts" (Rev. 9:20-21 KJV). The story is told of a monkey reaching into a jar with a narrow opening to grab an object. As long as he holds the object, he is trapped, because his fist cannot fit through the opening. How many people will hold on to their worthless idols until it is too late?

How many of these lies have you heard? Go to the church of your choice. You can worship any way you wish, just be sincere. There are many ways to God. Everyone has his or her own opinion. You should not force your religion on anyone. All of these lies have one thing in common. They are all essentially man-centered rather than God-centered.

First of all, the church is not real estate; it is people. We should be led by the Spirit of God as we join with other believers in a reciprocal relationship of giving as well as receiving. How can we worship God and not be interested in doing His will? There are not many ways to God. Jesus said, "I am the way, the truth, and the life: no man cometh unto the Father, but by me" (John 14:6 KJV). Unfortunately, though, there are many ways to hell and destruction.

While everyone seems to have their own opinion, they are deceived when they believe a lie. Proverbs 14:12 (KJV) says, "There is a way which seemeth right unto a man, but the end thereof are the ways of death." I once met a college professor who did not believe that man had traveled to the moon. He thought it was impossible. In his opinion, after spending millions of dollars, the government staged a movie with special effects showing a lunar landing. However, a person's opinion cannot put a flag on the lunar surface or remove a flag that is already there. The truth is not changed by opinion.

What does God say about "forcing religion" on people? Ezekiel 3:18-19 says, "If I warn the wicked, saying, 'You are under the penalty of death,' but you fail to deliver the warning, they will die in their sins. And I will hold you responsible for their deaths. If you warn them and they refuse to repent and keep on sinning, they will die in their sins. But you will have saved yourself because you obeyed me." Jesus said, "Go ye into all the world, and preach the gospel to every creature. He that believeth and is baptized shall be saved; but he that believeth not shall be damned" (Mark 16:15-16 KJV). This verse is often referred to as the Great Commission. It is not the great suggestion. The call to evangelism is made to all believers, not just "professional" clergy. It is our great opportunity to share the Good News of the Gospel and the love of Christ with those who are lost and so desperately need to hear the message of hope. When we enter into eternity, our opportunity for evangelism will end. How are we using such limited time to speak the name of Jesus, the One who loved us with such a great love? How much time do we spend in worship?

By contrast, how much time do we spend on entertainment, a substitute for worship? People often get incredibly defensive and angry when their worship is criticized. Many people have the attitude that worship is so personal that it is far beyond any kind of scrutiny. This attitude is certainly not restricted to contemporary society. Religious wars have been fought, and one major religion is said to be responsible for an estimated fifty to one hundred fifty million deaths. Cain, and then his brother, Abel, were the offspring of Adam and Eve. Abel was a keeper of sheep, and Cain was a tiller of the ground. Surprisingly, their very first record of worship in the Bible ended in murder.

We read their story in the fourth chapter of Genesis: "When it was time for the harvest, Cain presented some of his crops as a gift to the Lord. Abel also brought a gift—the best portions of the firstborn lambs from his flock. The Lord accepted Abel and his gift, but he did not accept Cain and his gift. This made Cain very angry, and he looked dejected" (Gen. 4:3-5). Admittedly, they brought the products of their vocation, and perhaps the best they had to offer. Yet, while God accepted Abel's offering, He did not respect Cain's offering. Hebrews 11:4 (KJV) says, "By faith Abel offered unto God a more excellent sacrifice than Cain, by which he obtained witness that he was righteous, God testifying of his gifts: and by it he being dead yet speaketh." This verse says Abel is still speaking. What is his message? May I suggest, God will respect our obedience to His Word. Man may be offended by God's judgment, but Cain was encouraged to get over it. God's Word says, "'Why are you so angry?' the LORD asked Cain. 'Why do you look so dejected? You will be accepted if you do what is right. But if you refuse to do what is right, then watch out! Sin is crouching at the door, eager to control you. But you must subdue it and be its master'" (Gen. 4:6-7).

Unfortunately, Cain let his rebellion and anger continue to fester and grow. Finally, Genesis 4:8 (KJV) says, "And Cain talked with Abel his brother: and it came to pass, when they were in the field, that Cain rose up against Abel his brother, and slew him." As people and societies rebel against God, their behavior and moral character will tragically disintegrate. The unmistakable evidence of this decline can be seen every day.

Being thankful is important. The book of Romans says, "Because that, when they knew God, they glorified him not as God, neither were thankful; but became vain in their imaginations, and their foolish heart was darkened" (Rom. 1:21 KJV). Throughout the chapter, the sinful and destructive behavior continues to sink. When people forget the blessings of God and become ungrateful, they will soon find themselves caught in a spiritual vortex.

Sadly, man has a history of only speaking to God in a time of crisis. It has been said that there are very few atheists in a foxhole on the battlefield. People cry out to God in times of need. The so-called "prosperity gospel" has encouraged its followers to pray and speak in a certain way to presumably release wealth and success. However, as a song I wrote a number of years ago says, "Men are needed who will seek God's face and not His hand."[1]

Then, there are people who are actually grateful to God. They look at a beautiful strawberry, a young kitten, a baby, or a sunset, and say, "Bless the name of the God who created all these things." Nevertheless, worship is more than being thankful. The Bible says in First Thessalonians 5:17 (KJV), "Pray without ceasing." As we go about our daily lives, we should go with God. A number of languages use "Go with God" as a greeting, but that is what we should really do. The Bible says we were created for fellowship with God.

However, true worship will extend far beyond material concerns to our fellowship with God, our love of God, and our appreciation of His grandeur and majesty. As we come to some realization of the holiness and nature of God, we will be in a better position to acknowledge our sinfulness and His tremendous love for us. Romans 5:8 (KJV) says, "But God commendeth his love toward us, in that, while we were yet sinners, Christ died for us." We should be so grateful to God for

His love. We should live each day in fellowship and adoration. He is the King of kings and Lord of lords. Hear the words of Revelation 5:13 (KJV): "And every creature which is in Heaven, and on the earth, and under the earth, and such as are in the sea, and all that are in them, heard I saying, Blessing, and honour, and glory, and power, be unto him that sitteth upon the throne, and unto the Lamb for ever and ever." Heaven is a place of worship. While most people plan to go to Heaven, very few are interested in worship.

Sadly, we live in a day similar to that of the prophet Isaiah, who said, "And there is none that calleth upon thy name, that stirreth up himself to take hold of thee: for thou hast hid thy face from us, and hast consumed us, because of our iniquities" (Isa. 64:7 KJV). I pray that as you read this book, and some of the books that Jennifer has referenced, you will be inspired to seek the face of God and worship God in spirit and in truth.

Ken Campbell

Introduction

"For this, O LORD, I will praise you among the nations; I will sing praises to your name" (Ps. 18:49).

In March 2019, the Lord awakened me one morning with the words, "Worship in spirit and in truth." Although it was not an audible voice, the Holy Spirit greatly impressed upon my heart the need for me to write this book. That very morning, I started writing the words within these pages, which I believe is a message the Spirit of the Lord is saying to the churches. Since that time, God has continually reminded me of this vital message. It seems the topic of worshiping God in spirit and in truth is prevalent now more than ever before. I have heard many different pastors repeatedly use these words in their sermons, and choirs have sung the lyrics, "We worship you in spirit and in truth,"[1] on many occasions since that special spring morning. The Lord has spoken to my heart countless times since I first felt a prompting in my spirit to write this manuscript.

Surely, the timeliness of this book is impeccable. When we examine the state of the world today, there is an imperative need for Christians around the world to worship the Lord continually, guarding against the evil forces, which seek to snuff out the bright lights we are shining for our Savior. As God's Word says, we need to be "making the most of every opportunity, because the days are evil" (Eph. 5:16 NIV). We must take every opportunity we have to worship Him and to share His marvelous love with others. It is time for Christians everywhere to lift up holy hands in praise to our Heavenly Father (1 Tim. 2:8). Worship cannot be a spectator sport. It is something each one of us must purposefully do, not just at church on Sunday, but every single day of our lives.

Jesus said, "'Yet a time is coming and has now come when the true worshipers will worship the Father in the Spirit and in truth, for they are the kind of worshipers the Father seeks. God is spirit, and his worshipers must worship in the Spirit and in truth'" (John 4:23-24 NIV). God is seeking true worshipers. Do you want God to seek you? Is your desire to please the Lord in all you do? Will you magnify His excellent name and worship Him wholeheartedly today?

I pray God will use the message in this book to challenge us to cast aside our earthly idols, putting God first in all we do. God created us to worship Him. Therefore, worship should be more than a weekly activity. Worship should be our way of life.

I am writing this book for one purpose and one purpose alone—to give all glory and honor to the King of kings and Lord of lords. Jesus Christ is the One whom I adore. He is the only One who deserves our praise. I invite you to join me in one accord. Let us worship Him in spirit and in truth!

Jennifer Joy Campbell

Chapter One

Created for Worship

"Bring all who claim me as their God, for I have made them for my glory. It was I who created them" (Isa. 43:7).

Bowing down, raising hands, singing praises—there are innumerable forms of worship throughout the world. Some groups worship on certain days of the week or during particular months of the year. There are people who believe they should only worship in a certain location and those who feel they have the freedom to worship anywhere in the world. While many individuals take worship very seriously, others are rather lukewarm in their approach to worship. The most important question concerning worship, however, is not how you worship, when you worship, or where you worship. The vital question surrounding worship is distinctly, "*Who* do you worship?"

Have you ever pondered what it really means to worship? According to the *Merriam-Webster Dictionary*, the word *worship* means "to honor or show reverence for as a divine being or supernatural power."[1] Although this is one of the correct definitions for this verb, the seemingly straightforward meaning of this word is rather complex. When it comes to a "divine being or supernatural power,"[2] this ambiguous reference could be addressing any number of prominent religious or even secular figures down through the ages.

Consider Mesopotamia, the region where the world's very first civilization was founded in Western Asia. The polytheistic Mesopotamians worshiped many different major gods and

1

thousands of minor gods, many of which are seldom regarded by modern civilization. Other religions continue to worship statues, animals, trees, and even people. People who worship these so-called gods are worshiping in vain. No individual on earth personally possesses the power to bring about miraculous healing or to give the gift of eternal life. Furthermore, a herd of animals or forest of trees cannot save a person, nor can an inanimate object bring salvation to someone's soul. We must look to the only living God, for He is the only One who can save us. He holds our lives in His hands. As Daniel said to Belshazzar, King Nebuchadnezzar's son, "'You praised the gods of silver and gold, of bronze, iron, wood and stone, which cannot see or hear or understand. But you did not honor the God who holds in his hand your life and all your ways'" (Dan. 5:23 NIV). Man-made idols could not save Belshazzar, for he was killed that very night (Dan. 5:30). We do not have to live in fear, for God has the power to help us in our human weakness. He is the only source of eternal hope. As my dad, Ken Campbell, wrote, "There is hope. There is light. There is salvation. His name is Jesus."[3]

The vital question surrounding worship is distinctly, "Who do you worship?"

Unfortunately, many people in this world are like Belshazzar, never recognizing God for who He really is. They are deceived to the point where worshiping other gods becomes an all-encompassing way of life, one that leads to a struggle for peace, a struggle for hope, and a struggle for life itself. As various groups attempt to fill the void in their hearts with worldly entities, they do not understand their inherent need for God. They overlook the possibility that there is only one true living God, who loves them more than they could ever begin to imagine. Individuals may instead seek solace in the fact they have a loving family, a lucrative job, or a comfortable home in which to live. No matter their lifestyle, they will one day realize that this world and all its pleasures can never fill the empty place deep within their soul.

The vacancy within a man or woman's heart is comparable to a children's jigsaw puzzle. No matter how hard you try, you will not likely be successful if you try to force a puzzle piece to fit into the wrong position. Likewise, nothing else in all of this earth will fill the void within a person's heart except the peace that comes from knowing Jesus Christ and the fellowship that is possible through His redemption. Ecclesiastes 3:11 (AMP) says, "He has made everything beautiful *and* appropriate in its time. He has also planted eternity [a sense of divine purpose] in the human heart [a mysterious longing which nothing under the sun can satisfy, except God]—yet man cannot find out (comprehend, grasp) what God has done (His overall plan) from the beginning to the end." God's plan for humankind is a plan of redemption, where the only way to achieve unprecedented peace is to surrender our lives to Him. The "longing" this verse speaks of can only be fully satisfied with redemption and relationship through our Lord and Savior, Jesus Christ.

Nonetheless, people often go to great lengths to find peace from other sources. Recently, I heard the story of someone who was suffering from alcoholism. They became so dependent on alcohol that their addiction nearly cost them their job. Sadly, some people cannot cope with the day-to-day challenges of life, which may cause them to desperately search for comfort in all of the wrong places. Although alcohol creates a chemical reaction in a person's brain that may temporarily ease their anxiety, the long-term, negative effects these substances have on an individual's mind and body, as well as their families and friends, certainly outweigh any fleeting, false peace they may experience during the time they are intoxicated. Yet, they treat their addiction as if it has the ability to save them from their distress. Instead of turning to the only One who can truly help them, Jesus Christ, they turn to the source of their problem for consolation, which only serves to complicate matters further and may even jeopardize their life.

From the very beginning, man has often been of the opinion that he knows best. Whether a person is consuming alcohol, or using illegal drugs, he or she often is under the impression that they have it all together. They are living their life, their way, on their own terms. The problem with this lifestyle is that it has no authentic outlook. If people only live for themselves, then they have no eternal hope for the future. Still, people rely on all sorts of things to try to gain knowledge of their future, from pagan rituals to gazing at the stars in the sky for an indication of what they should do and where they should go. While they are searching high and low for answers, engaging in immoral and even satanic activity, God has already provided the answers to all of life's questions in His Holy Word.

In contemporary society, consulting God's Word is no longer as admired as it used to be. In the United States of America, Bibles seldom find a place in children's book bags; even though our founders originally established the public education system to provide students the ability to read the Bible.[4] Additionally, the Ten Commandments scarcely grace the walls of courtrooms and other government facilities. Sadly, many people feel as if the Bible is old-fashioned and does not pertain to modern-day life. Isaiah 40:8 says, "'The grass withers and the flowers fade, but the word of our God stands forever.'" The Word of the Lord will never become obsolete. It is a life-changing book filled with messages from the Lord. It is not simply a chronicle of letters to ancient peoples, but a book of life-saving knowledge to everyone who reads the divine words written within its pages. God's Word is just as relevant today as it was one thousand years ago. It is God's message to us. God has given us this holy book as a guidebook for life. We cannot afford to ignore this priceless book, for it is a lamp unto our feet and a light unto our path (Ps. 119:105).

Instead of allowing the Lord to shine a light on their path, innumerable people are following the dark, worldly path of destruction. Among many groups of individuals, their desire to "fit in" exceeds any measure of common sense they may have. Some people would do anything, no matter how drastic the consequences, simply to achieve acceptance from another individual. They would risk their lives to please another human being, yet they disregard any notion that pleasing their Creator should be their primary goal in life. From immoral sexual behavior to murdering unborn children, this world has overwhelmingly rejected absolute moral direction. Wrong has become what is right, and what is right has become what is wrong.

> *The Word of the Lord will never become obsolete. It is a life-changing book filled with messages from the Lord. It is not simply a chronicle of letters to ancient peoples, but a book of life-saving knowledge.*

Isaiah 5:20 says, "What sorrow for those who say that evil is good and good is evil, that dark is light and light is dark, that bitter is sweet and sweet is bitter." God's Word says sorrow awaits those who attempt to turn evil into good, yet countless people are laser-focused on this wicked course. Society is in a downward spiral, and the underlying cause is easy to identify.

The majority of people living today do not want anyone telling them what to do. As a schoolteacher, I can tell you I have encountered students who were adamantly against all authority, from their parents all the way to the president. Many of them take the anarchist approach to life. Unfortunately, this non-authoritarian mentality will only result in a state of confusion. Romans 1:21-22 says, "Yes, they knew God, but they wouldn't worship him as God or even give him thanks. And they began to think up foolish ideas of what God was like. As a result, their minds became dark and confused. Claiming to be wise, they instead became utter fools." The apostle Paul was writing to the Romans around the year AD 57, but the same is true of the twenty-first century world population. Today, people generally do not respect authority, specifically God's authority.

I recently saw a post on social media where a person said they had been a Christian for thirty years, but they no longer believed in any form of a divine being. Based on further commentary from this very confused individual, they were unwilling to accept the truth that God was the One who created them. Instead of realizing their inherent need for God, they had the false impression that God was the One who had brought them to a place of apprehension, self-hatred, and insecurity. Just as the apostle Paul wrote in the book of Romans, this individual created irrational ideas in their mind concerning what God is like. Due to their darkened state, this atheist was certain that any improvement to their life since denouncing Christ was because of their own merit.

Simply knowing God is not enough. We must yield our lives to Him completely, in worshipful thanksgiving.

When we believe we can accomplish something solely on our own, we travel down the path leading to destruction. Although

we may make the decision to take on career-related tasks, family responsibilities, or personal goals, we could not even get out of bed in the morning if it was not for our Heavenly Father awakening us. Without God, we could not do anything. Without God, there would be no breath in our lungs. Without God, there would be nothing. Simply knowing God is not enough. We must yield our lives to Him completely, in worshipful thanksgiving. Only then will we be able to live a life of wisdom as opposed to imprudence.

We must take our eyes off the world and place our focus on worshiping the Lord God Almighty.

In Paul's writing to the Romans, he pinpointed the reasons the ancient Romans became unwise. There were two major errors on their part. They stopped worshiping God, and they stopped giving thanks to the Lord. Warren Wiersbe wrote concerning the transformation that took place within their minds: "Man the worshipper became man the philosopher, but his empty wisdom only revealed his foolishness."[5] These individuals believed they were wise like God, yet their incredulous nature toward God only created a society of unintelligent, self-seeking people who turned away from the only One who could save them.

When people start worshiping other people, their jobs, their homes, their automobiles, or anything or anyone other than God Himself, this will always be the beginning of the end. People cannot attain true, lasting contentment unless they put their trust in the Prince of Peace, Jesus Christ. All of the things this world has to offer can only provide temporary hope or momentary joy. Additionally, many of the immoral and illegal activities people engage in only lead to long-lasting, or even permanent, heartache.

Conversely, when we place our hope in Jesus Christ, we will receive the wondrous gift of eternal salvation and everlasting hope. We must take our eyes off the world and place our focus on worshiping the Lord God Almighty. Our purpose on this earth is to give all glory to the One who created us in His image!

The First Worshipers

"With my mouth I will greatly extol the LORD; *in the great throng of worshipers I will praise him" (Ps. 109:30 NIV).*

Upon the birth of the third generation of humankind, people began to call on the name of the Lord. One of Adam's grandsons, Enosh, was born in 3526 BC. Genesis 4:26 says, "When Seth grew up, he had a son and named him Enosh. At that time people first began to worship the LORD by name." For almost six thousand years, men and women have been crying out to our Heavenly Father for help in their time of need. What must it have been like for the first worshipers to call out to God? How did they feel when they took matters out of their own hands and placed their plight in the hands of God instead? More significantly, I wonder what God's response was when He first heard someone worshiping His holy name.

Although pondering questions like these causes us to think about the many complexities of God, we do not have to wonder what God thinks when someone is worshiping His holy name. First Corinthians 1:9 (NIV) says, "God is faithful, who has called you into fellowship with his Son, Jesus Christ our Lord." God is not sitting in Heaven, indifferent to whether we praise Him or not. Rather, He has called each one of us to worship the Lord. God desires for us to fellowship with His Son, Jesus. He wants us to commune with Him on a daily basis, sharing our sorrows and expressing our joys. He always wants to hear from His children.

God is not a divine being in Heaven who never stops to think about us. On the contrary, He is our Heavenly Father, attentively watching over us as a father would watch over his beloved children. Psalm 17:8 (NIV) says, "Keep me as the apple of your eye; hide me in the shadow of your wings." We are the apple of God's eye, created for His divine purpose. We are special in God's sight. Why else would He be concerned with the number of hairs on our heads? Luke 12:7 (NIV) says, "Indeed, the very hairs of your head are all numbered. Don't be afraid; you are worth more than many sparrows." The average person has approximately one hundred thousand hairs on their head, and God has numbered each individual one of them. God knows us much better than we know ourselves. We are a treasure in His sight, which is why we should devote our lives to serving Him. Our purpose on this earth is to give all glory to Him.

Revelation 4:11 (KJV) says, "Thou art worthy, O Lord, to receive glory and honour and power: for thou hast created all things, and for thy pleasure they are and were created." God created every man, woman, boy, and girl to worship Him. He did not create us so we could fulfill our duties at work, attend classes at school, clean the house, take a vacation, or enjoy a nice meal. Nor did He create us to live in a state of worry or fear. A.W. Tozer wrote, "Worship is man's full reason for existence. Worship is why we are born and why we are born again."[6] God created us for worship. Jeremiah 1:5 says He formed us in our mother's womb. Even before we were born, God made us in His image so we could bring Him joy and honor. He created us to worship Him and to please Him.

Perhaps the notion of pleasing God seems overwhelming to you. Do not dismay, for giving pleasure to God is within everyone's capability. In the book of First Thessalonians, the apostle Paul gave four simple directives on how we can please God in our daily lives. He said we should avoid immoral behavior, love one another, mind our own business, and work with our hands (1 Thess. 4:3-11). Everything we do should be pleasing to Him, from the relationships we have with our loved ones to the integrity and work ethic we display within our chosen careers. We should always be devoting ourselves to the central reason God placed us on this earth—to worship and honor God through everything we say and everything we do. Our constant desire should be to live a life pleasing to the Lord as we diligently strive to follow His divine will for our lives.

Regrettably, many people would rather follow their own path, participating in sinful acts and pursuing the things they personally think will make them happy. For some individuals, living a holy life seems as if it has too many strings attached. They would rather avoid following God's plan for their life, confident they can live a wonderful life without following His divine will. Nevertheless, they will one day realize that living against the will of God shall only lead to sorrow. When people ignore God's instructions, their life will frequently tailspin out of control.

Let us examine the lives of Cain and Abel, two of the sons of Adam and Eve. Abel was a shepherd. Cain was a farmer. They both offered a sacrifice to the Lord. Genesis 4:3-4 (AMP) says, "Cain brought to the LORD an offering of the fruit of the ground. But Abel brought [an offering of] the [finest] firstborn of his flock and the fat portions." When the Lord received these offerings, He was not pleased with Cain's offering, which stirred great anger within Cain's heart. Although they may have had different socioeconomic statuses due to their respective careers, it was not about the monetary value of the sacrifice, but the fact that Cain did not give his very best to the Lord. His meager sacrifice portrays a man who was an outright sinner in God's eyes, but Cain's antagonism shows he was oblivious to the fact that his offering was not "good enough." The Lord asked Cain, "'Why are you so angry? And why do you look annoyed? If you do well [believing Me and doing what is acceptable and pleasing to Me], will you not be accepted? And if you do not do well [but ignore My instruction], sin crouches at your door; its desire is for you [to overpower you], but you must master it'" (Gen. 4:6-7 AMP). God was telling him there was no future in a life of sin. Refusing to do what pleases God will only lead to ruin. On the contrary, living a life that glorifies God will result in full acceptance from the Lord.

Abel knew God deserved the very best, which is why he sacrificed one of his most valuable livestock, including the fat portions that were not for consumption but offered unto the Lord. Furthermore, Abel's offering was a blood sacrifice, which he offered to the Lord as atonement for his sins. Although the Bible only tells us that Cain had given "an offering of the fruit of the ground," we can infer that Cain did not offer the Lord a blood sacrifice or his very best sacrifice, considering God was not pleased with him (Gen. 4:3 AMP). Instead, God favored Abel's offering. Abel worshiped the Lord through his giving, withholding nothing from the Lord. Cain chose not to give the Lord a suitable offering, allowing his sinful nature to overrule what he most assuredly knew was honorable in God's sight. Cain's decision to preserve part of his wealth as opposed to worshiping the Lord wholeheartedly altered his life forever, leading him down an irreversible path of hatred and murder.

Because of his iniquity, Cain murdered his brother Abel out of jealousy, even though he was the one who chose not to worship the Lord with his very best sacrifice. To make matters even worse, Cain lied to the Lord by telling Him that he did not know where his brother was located following his murderous act (Gen. 4:9). Because the Lord is omniscient, He knew exactly what happened, but He sought a confession from Cain. Cain was so far away from God that he stopped at nothing to try to deny his evil ways. As Genesis 4:7 says, sin will wait at a person's door, in an attempt to subdue the individual to the point where they are powerless to let go of their wickedness. Temptation is easier to overcome at the door. Yet, Cain was so deep in sin there was nothing he could do to stop the evilness bound within his heart. Due to Cain's sinful ways, God cursed the ground he cultivated so he could never grow crops there again, and God made Cain a fugitive and a vagabond (Gen. 4:12). One terrible decision concerning his offering of thanksgiving to the Lord completely shattered his life, all because he failed to realize that God created us to live a life pleasing to Him, not to please ourselves.

God did not create us so He could have billions of robots running around on the earth. Revelation 4:11 says we were created for the Lord's delight. He created us so we could worship Him, even through our work. Colossians 3:23 (NIV) says, "Whatever you do, work at it with all your heart, as working for the Lord, not for human masters." Everything we do should be to serve the Lord with complete admiration. This means we should go to the office for the Lord, go to school for the Lord, and even clean the house for the Lord. There should never be a time when we are not living each moment in reverence to our Heavenly Father. God did not create us so we could find pleasure within ourselves, our family, our education, our careers, our finances, or any other thing on this earth. God created us in His image so we could exalt Him. Let us follow the example of Abel, who gave his premium possession as a sacrifice of praise. He wanted to revere the Lord through every aspect of his life, even through his giving.

God created us in His image so we could exalt Him.

Psalm 19:14 (NIV) says, "May these words of my mouth and this meditation of my heart be pleasing in your sight, LORD, my Rock and my Redeemer." We should all pray that our lives would be pleasing in God's sight. He is the One who has saved us, rescued us, and healed us. His love for you and me is so very great. Jesus Christ gave His life on a cross for the forgiveness of our sins. Surely, we should use our lives to honor Him in return. Romans 12:1 (NIV) says, "In view of God's mercy, to offer your bodies as a living sacrifice, holy and pleasing to God—this is your true and proper worship." Let us be emboldened in our faith, always giving our all to the cause of Christ, living a holy life pleasing in His sight. He deserves our very best. May God grant us the wisdom and the strength we need to overcome the enemy, always speaking words of life and pondering words of hope, for God created us to worship Him!

Chapter Two

Adore Him

"Thou shalt worship the Lord thy God, and him only shalt thou serve" (Luke 4:8 KJV).

*I*n 776 BC, the very first ancient Olympic Games took place in Olympia, Greece. Although the site largely lies in ruins today, visitors can still see where the Olympic cauldron receives the iconic flame during a special ceremony before the torch travels around the globe. This flame is a link between the ancient and modern Olympics. One summer, my dad and I had the opportunity to see the very spot where someone lights the torch. Additionally, we had the chance to stand on the starting line where the ancient Olympians would have lined up for their historic races. Stepping into the remains of the stadium, I realized the customs in place during the first Olympic Games would have forbidden me, as a woman, to enter the stadium during the various athletic events.

Even though modern customs have changed drastically since the days of the early Olympics, some things have not changed at all. During our visit to the Archeological Museum of Olympia, it was troubling to see the presence of literally hundreds of small man-made idols. Some of them were small enough to fit inside a coin purse, others would require a large suitcase in which to carry them, and a few of the marble statues would likely demand the use of some heavy machinery even to make them budge an inch. Of course, when we consider the fact that people originally created the Olympics as a festival to honor Zeus, their most important Olympic god, then the existence of such artifacts should come as no surprise. What astonished me the most, though, was the fact that some people today still revere these inanimate objects. One museum curator told visitors not to take a photo of one particular statute because it was highly regarded by many people. He was reverently concerned the statue might be offended by having its picture taken. It saddened me to witness firsthand the worship of man-made idols in our modern society.

For thousands of years, people have worshiped idols. From marble statues to golden calves, some individuals show no restraint when it comes to worshiping lifeless items. How could they believe that a piece of stone or metal could ever save them? I recall a time in the northern region of Spain, where we saw a statue representing the Virgin Mary, a popular figure in Christian iconography. More than one hundred years ago, this non-living object received the designation of a patron saint. Much to our dismay, we witnessed people continuing to worship this fabricated image even today. Having made the pilgrimage to this supposed holy site, they thought if they touched a portion of this idol, then they would receive a blessing. While idols are frequently associated with pagan religions, Christian themed idols are plentiful throughout the world. Contrary to their belief, inanimate objects do not have the power to bless, to heal, or to save. The people touching this statue needed to hear the words spoken by Samuel as he advised the Israelites: "'Do not turn away after useless idols. They can do you no good, nor can they rescue you, because they are useless'" (1 Sam. 12:21 NIV). Idols have no value whatsoever, extrinsically or intrinsically.

Nevertheless, history reveals that idol adoration has been a longstanding problem, even among individuals who knew worshiping man-made idols was a sin. Romans 1:21-23 (NIV) says, "For although they knew God, they neither glorified him as God nor gave thanks to him, but their thinking became futile and their foolish hearts were darkened. Although they claimed to be wise, they became fools and exchanged the glory of the immortal God for images made to look like a mortal human being and birds and animals and reptiles." Here we have individuals who knew the truth. They knew God, our Creator, yet they chose to exhibit foolish behavior when they began to worship man-made images instead of the one true living God. From the very onset of humanity, people have gone astray due to irrational ideas bolstered by their own misconstrued knowledge.

Look at the Israelites, for instance, when they were awaiting Moses' descent from the peak of Mount Sinai, where he received the Ten Commandments from the Lord. Instead of praying for Moses or worshiping the Lord, they gathered their gold together, so they could fashion a golden calf as an object of worship. Here the Lord had brought them out of bondage in Egypt, and this was how they showed Him thanks. The Lord told Moses, "Go, get thee down; for thy people, which thou broughtest out of the land of Egypt, have corrupted themselves: They have turned aside quickly out of the way which I commanded them: they have made them a molten calf, and have worshipped it, and have sacrificed thereunto, and said, These be thy gods, O Israel, which have brought thee up out of the land of Egypt" (Exod. 32:7-8 KJV). They readily changed the truth of God for a lie (Rom. 1:25). The Lord was enraged. He told Moses He would destroy these people because of their sinful conduct (Exod. 32:10). Moses pleaded with Him to spare the people, and the Lord chose to allow them to live.

While I understand Moses' desire to see the lives of the Israelites spared, I also suspect he was greatly ashamed of their unrighteous behavior. How embarrassing it must have been for Moses to have the Lord tell him that the people for whom he served as leader had turned their backs on God in this manner. This scenario is proof of how people can so easily lose their moral compass. Yet all it took was a few impatient people placing a suggestion in Aaron's ear to put this idol factory in motion.

They had grown tired of waiting for Moses to descend from the mountaintop. In an effort to alleviate their boredom, they sought to generate some form of entertainment, which could serve as a substitute for their leader Moses. They said to Aaron, "'Make us some gods who can lead us. We don't know what happened to this fellow Moses, who brought us here from the land of Egypt'" (Exod. 32:1). Aaron must have thought it was a good suggestion or else he had become weary of hearing the people complain. Either way, he gave in to their idolatrous ways. He told them to bring all of their gold jewelry to him and then he "took the gold, melted it down, and molded it into the shape of a calf" (Exod. 32:4). He saw how happy the people were to have this god to worship, so he decided to appease them even further by building an altar in front of the golden calf (Exod. 32:5).

The very idea that Moses' brother, Aaron, was helping the people engage in such pagan rituals is truly hard to fathom. Aaron was not some atheistic or agnostic individual who had never believed in God a day in his life. Quite the opposite, Aaron was one of the Lord's messengers, serving as the very mouth of Moses as they spoke to the Israelites and even to Pharaoh. What kinds of illogical thoughts ran through Aaron's mind as he fashioned a golden calf, so the people would have something to worship? Why did he cater to their wicked desires? How could he turn his back on the only true God by building a substitute god?

One determining factor might have been the high position of power this action afforded him. Aaron gained significant satisfaction from the creation of the golden calf. Not only did his actions serve to pacify the people, but it also placed Aaron in a position of authority. As he built the altar for this so-called god, he began to feel a sense of supremacy. Psalm 115:8 says, "And those who make idols are just like them, as are all who trust in them." While Aaron certainly knew in his heart that building an idol was wrong, his human desire to be the "savior" for the people overshadowed his ability to think clearly. Wiersbe wrote,

"You become like the god that you worship."[1] Upon seeing how pleased the people were, Aaron exclaimed, "'Tomorrow will be a festival to the LORD!'" (Exod. 32:5). The people were so eager for this festival; they awakened early in the morning "to sacrifice burnt offerings and peace offerings. After this, they celebrated with feasting and drinking, and they indulged in pagan revelry" (Exod. 32:6). Although their focus was ultimately not on the Lord, the people's gratification may have served to justify what Aaron had done, since he had been the primary source of their pleasure. Miserably, people often lose their moral direction when their human desire for recognition and power exceeds their ability to make sound decisions.

When Moses came down from the mountain, he was infuriated with the people for their ungodly behavior. Exodus 32:19-20 says, "He burned with anger. He threw the stone tablets to the ground, smashing them at the foot of the mountain. He took the calf they had made and burned it. Then he ground it into powder, threw it into the water, and forced the people to drink it." Moses was so angry that he took the sacred tablets, which he had just received from the Lord and threw them on the ground. Then, he turned to the person he had left in charge. He asked Aaron, his brother, "'What did these people do to you to make you bring such terrible sin upon them?'" (Exod. 32:21). Moses' first inclination was that someone must have coerced Aaron into manufacturing a golden calf, for surely his brother would not be so disobedient to God that he would perform such a horrid act by his own judgment. I am sure Moses was hoping Aaron would tell him that someone had betrayed him, holding him hostage and threatening to murder him if he refused to create an idol. Unfortunately, this scenario was not the case.

Aaron's response would almost seem humorous, except for the fact that there was nothing at all amusing about the situation. He answered Moses by relating the story of what had transpired while Moses was on the mountain, phrasing his words to sound as if the idol was an uncontrollable accident. Aaron said, "And I said unto them, Whosoever hath any gold, let them break it off. So they gave it me: then I cast it into the fire, and there came out this calf" (Exod. 32:24 KJV). At this point, I am sure Moses had heard enough. It is common knowledge that fire simply melts gold; for that reason, there is essentially no possible scenario where simply throwing gold into a fire would result in a sculpted calf emerging from the flames. Nevertheless, this is how Aaron tried to rationalize his absurd reaction to the people's impatience as he explained the event to Moses.

As I often tell my students, there are consequences for inappropriate conduct. In the case of the Israelites, the penalty for their idol worship was deadly. Moses asked those who were on the Lord's side to join him. All of the Levites gathered around Moses. They were instructed by God to "go in and out from gate to gate throughout the camp, and slay every man his brother, and every man his companion, and every man his neighbour" (Exod. 32:27 KJV). For the people who worshiped the idol and chose not to follow the Lord, their life came to an abrupt end because they turned their backs on God. Exodus 32:28 (KJV) says, "And the children of Levi did according to the word of Moses: and there fell of the people that day about three thousand men." Three thousand people lost their lives due to their disloyalty to God and their adoration of an idol.

Unfortunately, this is only one instance where thousands of people have died because of idolatry. When the Israelites were camping east of the Jordan River, "Some of the men defiled themselves by having sexual relations with local Moabite women. These women invited them to attend sacrifices to their gods, so the Israelites feasted with them and worshiped the gods of Moab" (Num. 25:1-2). These Israelite men knew God, yet this trap of seduction was too much for them to resist. Flavius Josephus wrote, "But the young men professed they would give them any assurance they should desire; nor did they at all contradict what they requested, so great was the passion they had for them."[2] These women had such power over the men that they were able to coerce them into agreeing to anything they suggested, even turning away from the one true God. The woman's response, according to Josephus, was, "'It will be absolutely necessary, if you would have us for your wives, that you do withal worship our gods. . . . Our gods are common to all men, and yours such as belong to nobody but yourselves.'"[3] Here we have a prime example of people who have no idea who God really is. These women have the mindset that the most common gods are the ones who deserve adoration. Yet, God is not the god of popularity. He is the only living God. As David wrote concerning the one true God: "It is you alone who are to be feared" (Ps. 76:7 NIV). Only the one true God deserves our adoration.

Detestably, these Israelite men traded the only living God for the counterfeit gods of these Moabite women.

May we all be like Joshua, casting aside all of the idols in our lives, as we confidently declare, "'As for me and my household, we will serve the LORD.'"

They worshiped Baal of Peor, "causing the Lord's anger to blaze against his people" (Num. 25:3). The term *Baal-peor* means "god of the opening." This god of the Moabites involved both conventional and deviant sexual behavior, which was a sin against God. God's anger came upon them through a directive delivered to Moses, who told Israel's judges, "'Each of you must put to death the men under your authority who have joined in worshiping Baal of Peor'" (Num. 25:5). The Bible clearly tells us that worshiping other gods is an abomination in the eyes of the

Lord. Here, God sent a plague upon these people, resulting in twenty-four thousand people losing their lives because they worshiped Baal instead of worshiping God (Num. 25:9).

When we place our focus on an idol, whether it be a statue created for the purpose of worship or any other aspect of life that we place before the Lord, such as a television, an automobile, a house, a career, or even our own family, we are in danger of losing our lives. Instead, we need to follow the advice of Joshua, who addressed all of the tribes of Israel when the Lord renewed His covenant with the Israelites. Joshua said, "'Now fear the LORD and serve him with all faithfulness. Throw away the gods your ancestors worshiped beyond the Euphrates River and in Egypt, and serve the LORD. But if serving the LORD seems undesirable to you, then choose for yourselves this day whom you will serve, whether the gods your ancestors served beyond the Euphrates, or the gods of the Amorites, in whose land you are living. But as for me and my household, we will serve the LORD'" (Josh. 24:14-15 NIV). We must throw the idols as far as we can, not just set them down. May we all be like Joshua, casting aside all of the idols in our lives, as we confidently declare, "'As for me and my household, we will serve the LORD.'"

Idol Adoration

"I hate those who pay regard to vain (empty, worthless) idols; But I trust in the Lord [and rely on Him with unwavering confidence]" (Ps. 31:6 AMP).

In modern times, nothing has changed when it comes to idolizing ungodly entities. Besides worshiping ancient artifacts from long ago, people engage in a wide array of idol worship in the twenty-first century. From idolizing other human beings to holding their wealth in high regard, individuals may worship other gods without even realizing the error of their ways. Recently, a teenager told me, "My cell phone is my life!" A declaration such as this may just be a hyperbolic statement from a young adolescent, but if this individual is genuine in these feelings toward their cell phone, they are essentially placing an electronic device in a higher position than God. Our lives are not dependent on technological wonders, but our acceptance of the wonder that the only true living God would love us so much that He would give His only Son as a perfect sacrifice for the atonement of our sins. Unfortunately, some people do not even know they need redemption, so the notion there is a God who loves them unconditionally is foreign to them. They go about their day, believing they are living their best life, never pondering the reality that they need a relationship with the Savior.

Rather than seeking the true and living God, some people are searching for answers in all of the wrong places. People may consult a psychic to find out what will happen in their future. They might look at astrological signs hoping to derive something from the galaxy, expecting to find direction for their next big move in life. Still others place their trust in a counterfeit god, which has no authority to rule over the heavens and the earth. All of these alternatives to Christ only serve to bewilder non-

> *Our lives are not dependent on technological wonders, but our acceptance of the wonder that the only true living God would love us so much that He would give His only Son as a perfect sacrifice for the atonement of our sins.*

believers as they fall prey to these pagan and cultic practices. When people turn their backs on Jesus Christ, they rapidly find themselves on a downward course of absolute destruction.

The Romans turned against the only living God, so God allowed them to engage in immoral sexual behavior and idolatry. The apostle Paul wrote, "Therefore God gave them over in the sinful desires of their hearts to sexual impurity for the degrading of their bodies with one another. They exchanged the truth about God for a lie, and worshiped and served created things rather than the Creator—who is forever praised" (Rom. 1:24-25 NIV). People have the same tendencies today. Instead of following God's laws for sexual conduct, they devise deviant forms of sexual behavior and immoral conduct. What's more, they publicly celebrate the countless ways they turn their backs on God's commandments. Not content with tolerance, they demand that society must celebrate their behavior. Rather than adhere to the truth, they formulate lies to try to convince themselves that their ungodly behavior is "normal." Instead of worshiping their Creator, they choose to worship a lie, or a false god, following the shameful example of many other deceived people groups down through the ages.

From the very beginning, men and women have believed the deliberate lies of Satan. In the Garden of Eden, the serpent deceived Eve by convincing her that eating the fruit would give her the infinite wisdom she so desired. In Genesis 3:1, the serpent asked, "'Did God really say you must not eat the fruit from any of the trees in the garden?'" Using a devious question, Satan placed doubt in her mind. Building upon this doubt, he said, "'God knows that your eyes will be opened as soon as you eat it, and you will be like God, knowing both good and evil'" (Gen. 3:5). The prospect of being able to know good and evil was too enticing to resist. She traded the only living God for a substitute god. Because she turned her back on God, God banned she and her husband from the garden and cursed the very ground they walked upon. One must ponder, what would have happened if Eve had not eaten the forbidden fruit? How would the world be different today if she had placed her hope in the one true God instead of giving in to Satan's evil scheme?

Lamentably, numerous people around the world still have a fixation with the forbidden fruits offered by Satan. Only these "fruits" do not always grow on a tree, for human hands create the majority of them. Instead of worshiping God, the Ephesians placed all of their hope in the Greek goddess Artemis. The entire city was an extremely wicked place, even to the point where people unreservedly conducted sexually immoral acts inside the temple built to honor their goddess. Many people made their livelihood from the sale of handcrafted idols, so they were not pleased when the apostle Paul came into town sharing the Gospel of Jesus Christ. Acts 19:9 says, "Some became stubborn, rejecting his message and publicly speaking against the Way." Even so, Paul persevered during the persecution, continuing to spread the Gospel message for two years in this area, "so that people throughout the province of Asia—both Jews and Greeks—heard the word of the Lord" (Acts 19:10). Paul's ministry in the city of Ephesus resulted in many people confessing their sins and accepting the Lord Jesus Christ as their Savior. Acts 19:18-19 (KJV) says, "And many that believed came, and confessed, and shewed their deeds. Many of them also which used curious arts brought their books together, and burned them before all men: and they counted the price of them, and found it fifty thousand pieces of silver."

Although God was moving mightily in this region, some citizens were not too thrilled over the vast number of people converting to Christianity. Demetrius, a silversmith who specialized in fashioning silver shrines of the goddess Artemis, was one of the most outspoken. He said, "'This fellow Paul has convinced and led astray large numbers of people here in Ephesus and in practically the whole province of Asia. He says that gods made by human hands are no gods at all'" (Acts 19:26 NIV). Demetrius is the prime example of someone who was deceived to the point where he could hear the truth and be completely deaf to the message of the Gospel. His desire to make a lucrative living, and not to desecrate the false goddess' prestige, outweighed any notion that the apostle Paul may actually be speaking of the only source of divine strength.

Demetrius was a victim of greed. Ephesians 5:5 says, "You can be sure that no immoral, impure, or greedy person will inherit the Kingdom of Christ and of God. For a greedy person is an idolater, worshiping the things of this world." Demetrius likely worshiped his money more than he worshiped Artemis, for his first priority seemed to be protecting his business venture. As a result, he made sure to tell the townspeople what Paul had said, strategically framing his paraphrase of Paul's words, which simultaneously served to promote his own handmade idols and to attack Paul. As soon as Demetrius delivered his devious dialogue to his fellow tradesmen, "They were furious and began shouting: 'Great is Artemis of the Ephesians!' Soon the whole city was in an uproar" (Acts 19:28-29 NIV). This altercation led to a riotous crowd, repeatedly chanting praises to the goddess of Artemis for two consecutive hours.

My dad and I have stood in the amphitheater where the riots broke out. We passionately declared, "Great is the God of the apostle Paul!" What a special moment it was to have the opportunity to worship the name above all names, Jesus Christ, in the midst of this place where pagan practices have been a regular occurrence for so many years. As we walked through the streets of ancient Ephesus, it was truly humbling to know we were retracing the steps of such a devout Christian like Paul. The opportunity to see where these biblical events took place was very moving. Yet, as we strolled through the streets of modern-day Kuşadası, Turkey, we were reminded how there are still innumerable people who need a transforming relationship with the true living God. We observed many individuals who sought solace from man-made customs and traditions.

Plastering nearly every marketplace was the image of a blue eye, which many people believe has the power to bring them good luck. Many people across the Mediterranean and throughout the continent of Asia consider this amulet to be a form of protection. Walking through the Grand Bazaar, hearing a call to prayer echo over the loudspeakers, I saw firsthand the great need for this country to know the only One who can save them. Sadly, less than one percent of the population in Turkey identifies as Christian. The majority of non-Christians in this region put their trust in inanimate objects and false gods, expecting these non-living entities to bring them eternal hope and salvation.

God does not share His glory with anyone.

Ever since the creation of the world, men and woman have fabricated a plethora of false gods, useless lucky charms, and other secularized sacred relics, which have no power whatsoever. Even within some prominent religions of the world, people cling to various material things, with the belief that these manufactured items will bring them divine intervention. Some of them even adopt the notion that the pastor or priest will be able to save them, completely overlooking the fact that these individuals are mere human beings just like themselves. In the midst of their confusion, they determine to worship the leadership, the artifacts, and even the church itself.

Having toured dozens of gothic style cathedrals in Europe, I can tell you these historic buildings are very different from the "house of prayer" that Jesus described (Isa. 56:7 KJV). As soon as you walk through the doors, you will often hear melancholic

pipe organ music and smell the scent of candles and incense lit to send prayers up to the heavens. Mummified bodies of saints are frequently on display. In front of them, people may kneel at an altar and pray to these earthly vessels left behind. The artistic adornments in many of these cathedrals would rival most any museum-curated collection of treasures. In one cathedral in Europe, they had a number of souvenir coin-pressing machines covered with LED lights, akin to something you would see in a picture of Las Vegas.

Still, the most ornate building on earth cannot save anyone. God is the only One who can save us from our sins. In a world filled with hopelessness, He is our only everlasting hope. Why should we desire to separate ourselves from the only One who can provide true redemption? People cannot save us, establishments cannot save us, and religions cannot save us. The fact that we need God in our lives is indisputable. Moreover, God must be the only One we serve, for we cannot serve more than one master (Matt. 6:24). God said, "You shall have no other gods before me'" (Exod. 20:3 NIV). God does not share His glory with anyone. He wants us to trust Him fully, surrendering our lives to His will. We cannot look to the world for guidance, for the things of earth will only lead us astray. We must place our complete faith in the One who created all things, the One who is God of the universe (Heb. 11:3).

> *Jesus Christ is the King of all kings and Lord of all lords. All other gods are counterfeit.*

We cannot afford to put our hope in anyone other than our Creator. No fabricated object, counterfeit god, or human being has any power to bless someone. Every single pagan and religious ritual is a disgrace if it does not give all glory, honor, and praise to the only true living God. Jesus Christ is the only One who can provide true prosperity, peace, and protection. Jesus said, "I am the way, the truth, and the life: no man cometh unto the Father, but by me" (John 14:6 KJV). Jesus Christ is the King of all kings and Lord of all lords. All other gods are counterfeit. Jesus is the only way to eternal life. He is the only One whom we are to worship and adore.

Chapter Three

The Heart of Worship

"Come, let us worship and bow down. Let us kneel before the LORD our maker, for he is our God" (Ps. 95:6).

*W*hen Jesus Christ was born, a group of Wise Men undertook a long, arduous journey to reach the house where He was living as a young child. They did not travel such a distance simply to see a little boy. The Magi asked, "'Where is the newborn king of the Jews? We saw his star as it rose, and we have come to worship him'" (Matt. 2:2). These individuals had one purpose for their expedition, and that purpose was to worship the King of kings and Lord of lords. They faithfully followed the star, which led them to their destination. Along the way, they did not become discouraged. They did not lose hope that they would actually be able to find Jesus, Mary, and Joseph. Nor did they fail to remember their reason for traveling so far.

God's Word says, "On coming to the house, they saw the child with his mother Mary, and they bowed and worshiped him" (Matt. 2:11 NIV). When they arrived, the first thing they did was to bow down and worship Jesus. After their tiresome trek, they did not complain about sore feet or aching muscles. Their minds were not on acquiring a hot meal, finding a place to bathe, or locating a bed on which to lie down. Likewise, they were not concerned with having a long conversation with Mary and Joseph. No one proceeded to present the gifts of gold, frankincense, and myrrh to the parents the moment they set foot inside the house. They stayed focused on their primary goal, and that was to worship the newborn King.

In the twenty-first century, we could take a lesson from the Magi. They trekked many miles in order to reach the place where Jesus Christ was living. On the contrary, some people nowadays find it a struggle to get in their air-conditioned automobile and drive to church every Sunday morning. They complain about the service being too early or running too late. When they arrive, they get upset if someone is "sitting in their pew." How would churches look different if believers joyfully walked through the doors, purposefully headed straight to the front of the church sanctuary, and wholeheartedly worshiped our Lord and Savior, Jesus Christ? What sort of impact would it have on our workplaces, schools, and other locations we visit throughout the week if we worshiped the Lord during our commute as well? Surely, making worship a priority would be a step toward pleasing the Lord in all we do (Col. 3:23). I am certain we would see a significant change in the way people interact with one another. Most assuredly, our testimony for Jesus Christ would have a much greater impact on those around us.

Furthermore, giving praise to the Lord would ultimately make a difference in our own lives. Look at the shepherds who came to see Jesus when He was born. In the book of Luke, we read about how they told others what they had witnessed. Luke 2:18 says, "All who heard the shepherds' story were astonished." They could not keep this Good News of great joy to themselves. Having knelt in the presence of the Almighty God was the most marvelous experience of their entire lives. When they shared their touching testimony of seeing Christ with their own eyes, other people were amazed at what they heard.

Like the shepherds, we should have the same reaction when we stand in the presence of the Lord. When we worship our Heavenly Father, we need to open our hearts, allowing God to change us from the inside out. This heartfelt worship will lead us to follow the will of God in our lives, and that is to love the Lord with all of our heart, all of our soul, and our entire mind (Matt. 22:37). By giving ourselves to Him, He can use us for His divine glory. Just as the shepherds were able to give testimonies of their encounter with Christ, we can have the same impact on people when we share with them what God has done in our own lives. It should not be a burden, or an embarrassment, to tell what the Lord has done for us; instead, it should be a desire we cannot suppress. It should be a joy.

Tozer once said, "No one can long worship God in spirit and in truth before the obligation to holy service becomes too strong to resist."[1] Our utmost desire should be worshiping our Heavenly Father and sharing His amazing love with everyone around us. Like an avid angler who restlessly looks forward to the next time they can cast their bait into the water, we should have an even greater longing to fish for souls (Luke 5:10). There should never be a time when we are not fully devoted to the Lord's service. When we put our trust in the one true living God, we should yearn to serve the Lord in all we do. No matter where God places us, we should take every opportunity to be witnesses for Christ. As Christians, we are all commissioned to share the Good News with the entire world (Mark 16:15). Part of fulfilling the Great Commission is to tell others what God has done for us, for that is what witnesses do. They tell what they have seen and heard.

When we put our trust in the one true living God, we should yearn to serve the Lord in all we do.

Imagine a witness standing before a judge, unwilling to share their eyewitness account of a crime they saw being committed. Instead, a witness should be quick to tell the truth, giving an honest report of what they have observed. Likewise, we should be eager to share encouraging testimonies of what God has done in our lives. We should be unable to refrain from telling everyone we meet about the marvelous love of Jesus Christ, which He lavishly bestowed upon us, whether we are speaking to the cashier at the local supermarket, the server at the café down the street, or our neighbor whom God has purposely placed right next-door to us. As Tozer said, serving the Lord should not be a chore, but an irresistible tugging at our heartstrings.

Personally, I cannot refrain from sharing the love of Jesus Christ, even with complete strangers. On one of our recent trips to New York, God gave my dad and me a divine appointment to speak to a Muslim family in Brooklyn. The meeting was quite unexpected, for many pieces of the puzzle had to fall into place.

> *We should be unable to refrain from telling everyone we meet about the marvelous love of Jesus Christ.*

As we were taking a walk one evening, one of my earrings fell off, slipping through a metal grate in the sidewalk. Although the earring was very inexpensive, its retrieval posed an interesting challenge. The next day, my dad fashioned a catch hook out of a couple of paperclips and attached it to a long thin audio cable, which we had with us. After several successful practice runs in our hotel room with the matching earring, he was able to retrieve my earring from a ledge on which it had fallen. As my dad was sitting on the grate, carefully pulling out the earring from many feet below, a woman approached us to see if we needed assistance. She said her family had experienced a flat tire, and it had been very difficult to put on the spare. Almost immediately, I also learned their child had been born prematurely, just like me. This common ground opened the door for a conversation that would soon become a thorough religious dialogue. Our conversations with this family lasted for nearly two hours, with me witnessing to my newfound acquaintance and my dad sharing the Good News with her husband.

Although they were practicing Muslims, the mother of the family seemed open to hearing about the Gospel. She said one of her coworkers attended The Brooklyn Tabernacle. I gave her a copy of my book, *When You're in the Sunset, There's Sunshine Awaiting You*. She told me she would definitely read it. I pray she has since read my testimony, so she can learn more about the truth of the Gospel of Jesus Christ, for it is my hope that I will see this precious family in Heaven one glorious day. If it had not been for my losing an earring and the family having car trouble, our paths would likely not have crossed. God is the One who orchestrated the opportunity to share the love of Jesus Christ with them. Since that night, I pray God has sent other Christians to water the seeds He chose us to plant, so this family will soon discover the truth of the only living God.

Although I often feel inadequate in confrontational situations like this one, where our conversations resembled an Islam versus Christianity debate at times, I know God is more than enough. No matter the circumstances, God will always give us the confidence we need to deliver the message, and He will even give us the words to speak. We only have to be willing to answer His still, small voice, by saying, "Yes, Lord, I will follow wherever you lead." Reflect back on the Wise Men and the shepherds. They did not know exactly what they would find when they followed the star. Nevertheless, they were compelled to follow the star and see what God had in store for them. They only knew they had a desire within their hearts to worship the Lord Jesus Christ. We need to have that kind of devotion. We need to have that level of trust. We need to step out on faith, with the knowledge that God will guide us all along the way.

While we may not be renowned theologians, the promise of Acts 1:8 says that the Holy Spirit will empower us to be witnesses of the love of Jesus Christ. God not only rules over the kingdoms of men (Dan. 4:17), He rules over our daily lives and activity.

In case you wonder if your life will ultimately change when you share your testimony with others, I can tell you that your life will never be the same again. For when "the shepherds went back to their flocks," they were "glorifying and praising God for all they had heard and seen" (Luke 2:20). Yes, they still had the same profession, but a change had taken place within their hearts. They were now fully in tune with the One who had created them. They were worshiping the Lord, even in the midst of the field among their sheep. Instead of bitterly enduring long hours tending sheep, they realized their purpose in life beyond the grassy fields. They knew God was the One who had miraculously sent His Son to earth, and they knew their calling was to tell others about the moment they saw our Lord and Savior face-to-face. The joy from their encounter with Jesus was too wondrous to contain. Much like the shepherds, may we all find ourselves in the position where we cannot resist sharing the Gospel of Jesus Christ with others, for there is no greater message we could ever convey.

Our Need for God

"For God so loved the world that he gave his one and only Son, that whoever believes in him shall not perish but have eternal life" (John 3:16 NIV).

When I was a little girl, a good friend of mine, Angie Hester, frequently sang a song titled, "People Need the Lord." Soon, I began singing the song myself because I realized the critical need for us to share the Lord's love with others. Written by Phil McHugh and Greg Nelson in 1983, the message of this song is still highly relevant today. When I peruse the headlines in the news, I am saddened at the current condition of the world. People slaughter millions of babies each year in the practice of abortion. Many are engaging in all kinds of immoral and deviant sexual activity. Cultural hatred and violence fill the earth. Surely, this world needs the Lord more than ever before. Without Him looking out for us, our lives would be on an irreversible course destined for destruction. It is only because of His matchless grace that the world does not come completely unraveled at its innermost core. In spite of His constant protection, many people reject God instead of worshiping Him, fully disregarding the fact that He is the One who created them.

Psalm 95:6-7 says, "Come, let us worship and bow down. Let us kneel before the LORD our maker, for he is our God. We are the people he watches over, the flock under his care." God, in His infinite wisdom, intricately designed every human being on this earth. He wants to watch over us and protect us, but we must first worship Him and bow down before Him. The majority of the world is adamantly against worshiping Jesus Christ, yet He is the only One who can save us. God is not a man-made entity or human being who will disappoint us. He is the only living God, the One who created us. He holds all power in His hands. He is the One who hung the stars in place. I know firsthand that God is perfectly capable of protecting every human being on earth, just as a shepherd watches over his sheep.

If God had not been watching over me on the day I was born, I would not be alive today. When I came into this world, the medical world gave up all hope for my survival. On January 2, 1982, I was born prematurely and without a heartbeat. The doctors and nurses laid me aside, and they told my parents there was nothing they could do. My parents prayed in faith, "Jesus, help." Soon they heard what sounded like a little kitten start to cough. I was alive. Although I endured heart surgery at seven days old and spent several weeks in the neonatal center, God spared my life. He is the reason I am alive today. I give Him all of the glory, honor, and praise.

God did not heal me because my parents hoped He could be of assistance. Nor did God heal me because of anything the doctors and nurses did that evening. God healed me because of His sovereign grace. My mom and dad knew that no person, organization, or religion could restore my life. They put their trust in Jesus Christ, the only One who can heal us, restore us, and save us. They did not just *say* a prayer; they prayed in faith. Just as my parents called on the precious name of Jesus, we must ask the Lord for help and surrender ourselves to Him. Jesus said, "'Ask and it will be given to you; seek and you will find; knock and the door will be opened to you'" (Matt. 7:7 NIV). If we do not ask, we may never receive. If we do not seek, we may never find what we need. If we do not knock, the door may never open for us. My parents asked in faith for God to restore my life, and He answered their humble prayer.

When we bring our needs to God, He will grant us mercy and grace. Hebrews 4:16 (NIV) says, "Let us then approach God's throne of grace with confidence, so that we may receive mercy and find grace to help us in our time of need." Unfortunately, there are people in the world who do not like to ask for help. They would rather stand precariously on a chair to reach something as opposed to asking someone taller to assist them. Someone may prefer missing church rather than ask another individual to pick them up and drive them when their car is in the shop. Others miss many blessings because they do not want to be a bother, refraining from asking a friend to shop for their groceries, mow their lawn, or even share a meal with them. Likewise, people are often wary of asking God for something; for fear that He will either think it is too trivial of a problem, or conversely, too massive of a request. As a result, they spend their days continuously trying to decide what is an "okay" request to bring to God. Yet the scripture does not say to only approach

God if you have a worthwhile reason; it just says we should approach God with confidence.

God's love extends to the homeless person living on the street as well as the world-renowned preacher. God is not a respecter of persons (Deut. 10:17). He will hear His children when they pray. He wants us to come to Him with all of our needs. First Peter 5:7 says, "Give all your worries and cares to God, for he cares about you." God does not want us to be anxious. He wants us to rely on Him in every aspect of life.

My dad and I consider it a blessing to have traveled to over fifty-five countries and territories. In our travels, we have encountered many people who looked downcast, some who felt unloved, and others who were nearly ready to give up on life itself. What a privilege it has been to tell them about the hope we have in Jesus Christ. To be able to share the greatest message of all is truly a tremendous responsibility, one that could change the course of their lives forever. When they come to the realization that Jesus Christ loves them more than they could imagine, their lives will never be the same again. The knowledge that God, our Creator, cares for them in such a special way has the power to transform the most discouraged mind, the most detestable heart, and the most drained spirit. Moreover, the acceptance of the only living God who loves them unconditionally is the only thing that can fill the void within their heart.

God has placed an innate need in each one of us to worship our Creator.

God has placed an innate need in each one of us to worship our Creator. Nevertheless, many people disregard this tugging at their heart, assuming they can call on God at some other time.

They make excuses, saying they will call on the Lord next month when they have some vacation time or next year when they get their finances in order. They may put up an affront, saying they have no need for God, thinking they have everything figured out on their own. When they encounter a difficulty on the road of life, either they react despondently with no hope in sight or they cling to God, but for a moment, until the storm has passed. These calamity-induced Christians completely miss the point of Christianity altogether. While calling on God in the midst of their trials can bring them some level of comfort, they miss all of the blessings the Lord wants to pour out on them every day of the year. Additionally, some of the people who call on God only in the middle of tragic circumstances deceive themselves into thinking they have a relationship with Him, even though they have never confessed their sins or put their trust fully in Jesus Christ.

Jesus Christ is the only way to have a true relationship with God.

Simply calling on Jesus in times of trouble will not save your soul. The Bible says we have all sinned, which means we are all in need of salvation (Rom. 3:23). Jesus Christ is our Savior. Romans 10:9 (NIV) says, "If you declare with your mouth, 'Jesus is Lord,' and believe in your heart that God raised him from the dead, you will be saved." Salvation is a gift to all who will believe. When someone confesses their sins and believes that Jesus Christ is Lord, then they will receive salvation. There is no other way to receive this eternal treasure. You cannot earn salvation. No amount of good deeds or monetary donations can earn you entry into Heaven. Jesus said, "'I am the way and the truth and the life. No one comes to the Father except through me'" (John 14:6

NIV). Jesus Christ is the only way to have a true relationship with God.

Throughout my lifetime, God has blessed me with many dear friends and family members. I rejoice in the fact that many of them, before they went to be with the Lord, knew Jesus Christ as their Lord and Savior. Because of this fact, I have complete assurance that I will see them again one joyous day in Heaven. Unfortunately, I am uncertain as to the salvation of some of their souls before they departed this earth. I pray they called on the name of Jesus Christ before they drew their last breath. Sorrowfully, some people determine to wait until a more convenient time to call on Jesus Christ. Yet, James 4:14 (NIV) says, "Why, you do not even know what will happen tomorrow. What is your life? You are a mist that appears for a little while and then vanishes." Surely, we have no guarantee of tomorrow, which is why we need to make things right with God today.

In this modern age, people often focus on living out their own plan for their lives, unwilling to admit their need of the Savior. While they may carve out an hour a day to attend a church service, they never even consider the notion of daily worshiping the One who gives us life. People often feel the idea of humbling themselves and raising their hands in worship is going too far. What if Jesus Christ had thought being beaten beyond recognition, having nails driven into his hands and feet, and dying on a cross for the forgiveness of our sins was "going too far" for sinners like you and me? He left His throne in Heaven to come to this wicked

We have no guarantee of tomorrow, which is why we need to make things right with God today.

world filled with disobedience toward God. He came to seek and save the lost (Luke 19:10). The Bible says Christ died for us when we were still sinners (Rom. 5:6). He came to bring salvation to all who will believe. The name of Jesus means, "The LORD is salvation" (Matt. 1:21 AMP). Jesus came to save us. Surely, we could at least take a few moments each day to thank Him by giving Him the praise He so greatly deserves.

Unfortunately, many people do not want to adore the King of kings and Lord of lords. It is saddening to see the number of people who are adamantly against worshiping a higher authority. Instead, they want to worship entities created by man. Whether it is a cartoon character, an electronic gadget, a celebrity figure, or an athletic team, people find an infinite number of idols in which to put their hope. Yet nothing made by any human being on earth can ever provide eternal hope. Jesus Christ, our Lord and Savior, the One who gave His life for us, is the only source of everlasting hope. Nothing and no one can ever change this glorious fact. Why should we desire to worship anyone or anything else? Our complete adoration should go to the only One who can truly help us in our time of need. He is the only One who can rescue us. He is the only One who can save our souls.

This is the heart of worship: surrendering ourselves to the only living God, trusting Him as a child would trust their loving father.

We all need the daily presence of the Lord in our lives. Just as my parents cast all of their cares on Jesus, putting all of their trust in the name above all names, Jesus Christ, on the evening when I was born, we must surrender our all to Him. He is the only One we are to worship and adore. This is the heart of worship: surrendering ourselves to the only living God, trusting Him as a child would trust their loving father. We cannot worship the Lord wholeheartedly until we take ourselves out of the picture. According to Tozer, "The essence of surrender is getting out of the way so that God can do what He wants to do."[2] Worship should never be about us, but it should always be about Him. Jesus Christ should always be the center of our worship. Let us sincerely worship Him for all eternity!

Chapter Four

The God We Know

"And we know that the Son of God has come, and he has given us understanding so that we can know the true God. And now we live in fellowship with the true God because we live in fellowship with his Son, Jesus Christ" (1 John 5:20).

Corrie ten Boom once said, "Never be afraid to trust an unknown future to a known God." During her lifetime, the Second World War raged on, and she and her family risked their lives to provide a safe haven for Jewish families during the Nazi Holocaust. Through their heroic actions, God used them to save the lives of hundreds of individuals. As she and her family served as a refuge during the Holocaust, their future was very uncertain. One word, one mishap, and they could have all been arrested and lost their lives at the hands of the Nazi regime. Yet, through all of the strife she endured, ten Boom kept her faith in God. She knew God would never fail. God was not a faraway divine presence in her life, but someone she trusted, someone she loved, and someone she knew.

Surely, we should all have this same level of trust in our Heavenly Father. He loves us more than we could ever imagine. When we put our trust in Him, we become His children. First John 3:1 says, "See how very much our Father loves us, for he calls us his children, and that is what we are! But the people who belong to this world don't recognize that we are God's children because they don't know him." Individuals who have not yet put their trust in the one true living God do not have this same intimate relationship. The Bible says straightforwardly, "They don't know him." It is not that they are a new Christian and are developing a relationship with Him; instead, they do not know Him at all. These non-believers cannot call on our Heavenly Father as a child would call out to their father or mother. He is a stranger to them. For many people, their first prayer should be a prayer of repentance, for their sins separate them from God. Isaiah 59:1-2 (NIV) says, "Surely the arm of the Lord is not too short to save, nor his ear too dull to hear. But your iniquities have separated you from your God; your sins have hidden his face from you, so that he will not hear." Until an individual calls on God for mercy, He will not listen to their prayers. Only when they humbly repent can they truly know God.

Personally, I could not imagine only being able to call on an unknown god. Think about it. What if you could no longer call your friends or family for help, but you were only able to call on a complete stranger, living in an undisclosed location, uncertain as to whether or not they would even answer your call? I am sure many of us would give up very quickly, as this would seem like a hopeless situation. Many people are living this way today, calling on someone whom they do not know. They are like the Samaritan woman to whom Jesus said, "'You Samaritans worship what you do not know'" (John 4:22 NIV). Likewise, many people worship an ambiguous god. They do not know the location of their god, and they are not even sure if their god will hear them when they pray. Some people know *of* a god, but they do not personally know the one true God.

Some people know of a god, but they do not personally know the one true God.

In the Bible, we read of the Athenians who worshiped God,

yet knew not who He was. In Acts 17:23 (KJV), the apostle Paul said, "For as I passed by, and beheld your devotions, I found an altar with this inscription, TO THE UNKNOWN GOD. Whom therefore ye ignorantly worship, him declare I unto you." Here an entire group of people was very religious, devoting their lives to worshiping many things, including God. Nevertheless, they had no clear picture of who God was; their complete notion of there being one true living God was missing. Rather than worshiping Him as the only living God and embracing His unconditional love, they placed Him on a pedestal beside their other gods. Their idea of worship was to honor all of their gods, but not to actually have a meaningful relationship with the only living God.

God does not want us to place Him on a shelf alongside other idols in our lives, only to seek Him on Sundays.

Unfortunately, this type of worship is all too common in the twenty-first century. Many people seek to honor God, while keeping Him at a distance. Regardless of the desire some people have to practice a hands-off approach to worshiping God, the Bible clearly states that we are to worship Him on a personal level. God is seeking true worshipers who will worship Him in spirit and in truth (John 4:23). As an alternative to worshiping God in spirit and in truth, some people follow the example of the Athenians, worshiping an entire collection of idols. They place Him among a group of alternative gods, as if one god may not be enough. In modern times, people are not only worshiping statues, but they also put people, places, and things ahead of God as they attempt to prioritize their lives in vain. We must give God precedence in our lives. God does not want us to place Him on a shelf alongside other idols in our lives, only to seek Him on Sundays.

Exodus 34:14 (NIV) says, "Do not worship any other god, for the Lord, whose name is Jealous, is a jealous God." God has no desire to be one of many gods in our lives. He wants us only to worship Him. Isaiah 42:8 (NIV) says, "'I am the LORD; that is my name! I will not give my glory to anyone else, nor share my praise with carved idols.'" Disregarding the Lord's commands, the Philistines brought a plague of tumors upon the town of Ashdod and surrounding regions when they placed the Ark of the Covenant inside the pagan temple next to the idol of Dagon (1 Sam. 5:1-12). God does not share His splendor with anyone or anything. As Joshua said to the Israelites, "'Now fear the LORD and serve him with all faithfulness. Throw away the gods your ancestors worshiped beyond the Euphrates River and in Egypt, and serve the LORD'" (Josh. 24:14 NIV). Proverbs 9:10 (NIV) says, "The fear of the LORD is the beginning of wisdom." If we want to be wise in God's eyes, we will faithfully worship the Lord. God has no desire for us to worship Him only one day a week, while we serve other gods the rest of the week. He only wants us to have a relationship with Him. God requires us to be faithful to Him, just as He is faithful to us.

Likewise, God does not want us to act as if we are perfect strangers, never seeking His will for our lives or coming to Him with our concerns. He is our Heavenly Father. God desires for us to spend time with Him on a daily basis, desiring to develop a familiarity with Him, getting to know Him better every day. Christ did not die on the cross so we could sit in a church pew for one hour each week. He wants us to put Him first in our lives, worshiping Him with thanksgiving. When we put Him first, then we will find that everything else falls perfectly into place, according to His divine will for our lives. On the contrary, if we do not put Him first, we will find that everything falls into discord. Jesus said we should not even worry about what we should eat or what we should wear. He said, "'But seek first his kingdom and his righteousness, and all these things will be given to you as well'" (Matt. 6:33 NIV). The key to living a worshipful life is to seek the Lord first. We must recognize the fact that we cannot do anything on our own, but only through the grace of God. A life in tune with God will have perfect harmony, along with the goodness and mercy that only come from knowing our Father in Heaven. We must move past merely acknowledging God and devote ourselves to actually nurturing a close relationship with God.

Knowing God is not a guessing game, nor is it a privilege reserved for a select few. Everyone has the opportunity to develop a life-changing relationship with God. However, He does not force Himself on anyone. We must choose to take the first step toward getting to know Him on a personal level. That first step is to believe in His only Son, Jesus Christ. Once we put our trust in Jesus, then God will provide us with everything we need to live a life pleasing to Him. God's Word says, "By his divine power, God has given us everything we need for living a godly life. We have received all of this by coming to know him, the one who called us to himself by means of his marvelous glory and excellence" (2 Pet. 1:3). Each one of us must make a resolute decision to come to God humbly, surrendering our lives to His sovereign will.

Furthermore, we must fully determine in our hearts to acknowledge His greatness on a continual basis. God is not someone whom we should only come to when we have a personal need. As Second Peter 1:3 says, God calls us to come to Him through "his marvelous glory and excellence." We cannot afford to worship God only when we need something. Instead, we must recognize the fact that God is more than a provider of our needs. He is excellent. He is so loving. He is most holy. He is beyond all other gods. He is most worthy of our praise. If we solely worship Him for what He does, we will forgo the precious opportunity to have an intimate relationship with our Creator.

Instead, we need to realize the value of worshiping God for who He is. He is our Father in Heaven. He watches over us daily, pouring out His mercies anew every morning (Lam. 3:23). When we develop a sincere relationship with Him, our lives will change forever.

Knowing the one true God on a deeper level will not only change our lives in the here and now, but coming to know our Heavenly Father will transform our lives for all eternity. John 17:3 says, "And this is the way to have eternal life—to know you, the only true God, and Jesus Christ, the one you sent to earth." When we come to know God, we will approach life with a completely different perspective because we will "have this hope as an anchor for the soul, firm and secure" (Heb. 6:19 NIV). By placing our trust in the one true living God, we will no longer be afraid of what tomorrow may bring because of the eternal hope only found through Christ. We will always have someone on whom we can call. We will be able to trust our unknown future completely to a known God who loves us more than we could ever comprehend.

God With Us

> *"Behold, a virgin shall be with child, and shall bring forth a son, and they shall call his name Emmanuel, which being interpreted is, God with us" (Matt. 1:23 KJV).*

When we consider the need for everyone to know God, we must also examine the fact that a relationship with God requires more than simply knowing about Him. I can know about the prominent leaders of the world, but still not know them. I can search the Internet and discover the names of their children and even their grandchildren. I can know whether they have a pet, what kind of books or music they enjoy, and if they prefer water, coffee, or tea. Yet, all of this information means nothing, for knowing random facts about other people does not mean you personally know them. This is evident when Jesus performed a miracle in the life of a man possessed by a demon. The impure spirit said to Jesus, "'I know who you are—the Holy One of God!'" (Luke 4:34 NIV). This unclean spirit was about as far away from God as possible, yet still knew about the holiness of our Savior. Even the evil serpent in the Garden of Eden spoke of God when he tempted Eve to eat of the tree of the knowledge of good and evil, as Satan used this serpent to bring sin and rebellion into the world (Gen. 3:1-7). In the words of Martin Luther, "The serpent is a real serpent, but one that has been entered and taken over by Satan."[1] Revelation chapters twelve and twenty also describe Satan as "that old serpent" (Rev. 20:2). Satan did not have a loving relationship with God, but only knew of Him.

Furthermore, Pilate, the man who handed Jesus over for Crucifixion, must have known that Jesus was who He said He was. John 19:19 (KJV) says, "And Pilate wrote a title, and put it on the cross. And the writing was JESUS OF NAZARETH THE KING OF THE JEWS." When the chief priests saw this placard, they told him he should only write that Jesus claimed He was the King of the Jews (John 19:21). Instead of implementing their suggestion, Pilate said, "What I have written I have written" (John 19:22 KJV). Unfortunately, Pilate is not alone in his position of acknowledging the prominence of Jesus Christ, yet having no idea within his heart who He really is. Millions of people know of Jesus, but they do not know Him in a personal way. The knowledge of God is not enough. In order to grow a meaningful relationship with God, we must be more than acquaintances with our Father in Heaven.

What if you only knew the names of your parents, grandparents, or children, and you had never spent even five minutes getting to know them? Additionally, let us imagine that you had never enjoyed a meal with them, gone on a family outing together, or even lived under the same roof. Surely, this would result in a group of perfect strangers who just happened to be relatives. The same would be true of a husband and wife who had never shared an intimate conversation, or a grandparent and grandchild who had never enjoyed one another's company. I am so grateful that God has given me a loving daddy who I can talk to about anything, always ensuring that we have a close father-daughter bond. Yet, if we had never even seen each other or spoken to one another, we would have no familial connection at all. Unless we spend quality time together, we cannot develop authentic relationships with our loved ones. Likewise, when we do not spend time in fellowship with God, we cannot cultivate a genuine bond with the One who created us.

Moreover, there are people in the world today who are like the woman at the well, awaiting the arrival of the Messiah, oblivious to the fact that He lives among us. In her situation, she did not even have to have faith, for He was standing directly in front of her, speaking to her face-to-face. Instead of recognizing Jesus as the Christ, she questioned His request for a drink of water, since He was a Jew speaking to a Samaritan woman. Jesus responded, "'If you knew the gift of God and who it is that asks you for a drink, you would have asked him and he would have given you living water'" (John 4:10 NIV). Jesus acknowledged the fact she did not know who He was; her inability to discern His identity is because she seemed to know more about religious teaching than she knew about Jesus Himself. She said, "'I know that Messiah' (called Christ) 'is coming. When he comes, he will explain everything to us'" (John 4:25 NIV). Here she made a declaration of waiting for the Messiah while simultaneously speaking to Him. Her lack of understanding is disheartening to read, considering the millions of people today who have been in the presence of the Lord, yet likewise fail to recognize His splendor and majesty. As Jesus said to the Samaritan woman, He is saying the same to us today: "'I, the one speaking to you—I am he'" (John 4:26 NIV). Jesus Christ is the Messiah. He is the Son of the only living God. He wants to give us living water. He wants us to recognize Him when we are in His presence. He wants us to know Him, so we can sincerely worship Him in spirit and in truth.

First John 5:20 tells us how we can experience sincere fellowship with God through coming to know His Son, Jesus Christ: "And we know that the Son of God has come, and he has given us understanding so that we can know the true God. And now we live in fellowship with the true God because we live in fellowship with his Son, Jesus Christ. He is the only true God, and he is eternal life." We must first come to know God's Son, Jesus Christ, if we want to have a genuine relationship with our Father in Heaven. Jesus said, "I am the way, the truth, and the life: no man cometh unto the Father, but by me" (John 14:6 KJV). Unless we call on the precious name of Jesus, we will not gain access to His Father. Knowing Jesus is a prerequisite to knowing God. Once we accept Jesus Christ as our Lord and Savior, then we can dwell in the presence of the Almighty. In order to experience God's presence, we must be present. Meaningful fellowship with God requires us to set aside time for communion with Him.

In order to experience God's presence, we must be present.

Unfortunately, much of the communication people have with God is one-sided. A popular belief in the world today is that God is the god of fulfilling our desires. In other words, people come to Him with a wish list, if you will, telling God what they need and what they want. As soon as we have uttered our last

request, we go on about our day, never talking to the Lord until our next need arises. We are sometimes like children who knock on the door and run away. The greatest fallacy in this approach to a relationship with God is that we miss one of the most important aspects of knowing God. Instead of only speaking to the Lord, we should also spend quality time listening to His voice as He speaks to our hearts. People often say they wish they could hear God speaking to them. My response to them would be, "Read the Bible." My dad says if you want to hear God speak in an audible way, read the Bible aloud. God's Word is a message from God to us. He speaks to us every day through the Scriptures, but only if we take time to study and read His Word. Just as a nutritious meal only provides nutrition upon consumption, the Bible only feeds us spiritually when we meditate on the wisdom of God's Word. Wiersbe wrote, "The better we know the Word of God, the better we shall know the God of the Word."[2] God's Word is our guidebook to life, revealing God's master plan for our lives.

Until we make knowing God a priority, we will never fully know our Creator.

The apostle Paul wrote, "All Scripture is God-breathed and is useful for teaching, rebuking, correcting and training in righteousness, so that the servant of God may be thoroughly equipped for every good work" (2 Tim. 3:16-17 NIV). God has given us His Word as a tool, which we can use to help us navigate the tumultuous waters of this journey called life. He has given us instruction for every facet of our lives, but if we never read the Scriptures, how can we expect God to speak to us? Consider a patient seeing a doctor for an ailment. If they receive some medication to help them get well, but never use even one dose, how can they expect it to do any good? The majority of Christians take this same approach to reading the Bible. They think having a Bible app on their smartphone or a Bible on their nightstand will somehow have a positive influence on their lives. Contrary to their belief, a Bible gathering dust will not bring any spiritual refreshment on its own. Charles Spurgeon once said, "A Bible that's falling apart usually belongs to someone who isn't." Only when we actively open God's Word and meditate on the Scriptures will we find encouragement and divine guidance. When we take time to read the Bible and to listen to His voice, then we can gradually nurture a greater understanding of God Himself. Until we make knowing God a priority, we will never fully know our Creator.

Perhaps you are wondering how you could ever come to know God, since He is sitting on His throne in Heaven. Unlike some people we know who live a long distance away, Jesus is as close as the mention of His name. Acts 17:27 says He is "not far from any one of us." We can pray and seek His presence every single day, no matter where we are. Unfortunately, some people do not grasp this concept. Rather, they spend countless hours pondering how they can find God. They even engage in heated discussions of where people should worship. From rural church houses to city cathedrals, the places of worship are as diverse as the worshipers who attend them. Meanwhile, everyone seems to have his or her own perfect notion of the proper setting for worship.

Even the Samaritan woman whom Jesus spoke to said, "'Our ancestors worshiped on this mountain, but you Jews claim that the place where we must worship is in Jerusalem'" (John 4:20 NIV). This woman believed the mountain was the location from which she should worship, not because the Holy Spirit led her to that place, but because she was following the lead of her ancestors. This mentality is akin to the people in churches today who constantly say things like, "That's the way we've always done it." While it may be beneficial to keep some long-standing church traditions alive, there should also be room for adjustments. In addition to her knowledge of the worship customs of her ancestral heritage, she was also aware that the Jews worshiped in Jerusalem. Jesus said to the Samaritan woman, "'Believe me, a time is coming when you will worship the Father neither on this mountain nor in Jerusalem'" (John 4:21 NIV). As opposed to telling her where to worship, Jesus told her the two places she referred to as places of worship would no longer be the locations where people would gather to honor the Lord. Instead, He said the time had "'come when the true worshipers will worship the Father in the Spirit and in truth'" (John 4:23 NIV). Notice He did not say the worshipers would worship in a church sanctuary, at a special holy site, or other predetermined location. Jesus plainly told her, "'True worshipers will worship.'"

While there is much debate as to where a person should go to worship, the Bible gives us clear indications that finding the ideal place of worship does not begin with typing GPS coordinates into a tracking device, but with a focused heart set on worshiping God. If we are worshiping in spirit and in truth, our current position on the global map will bear no weight in how successful we are in reaching the throne of grace. Worshiping the only living God is not something we can only do in a certain location on a specific day of the week. Psalm 96:9 says, "Worship the LORD in all his holy splendor. Let all the earth tremble before him." This verse reaffirms the fact that we should not worry about when, where, or how we worship the Lord, but whether we actually worship Him. As we see the global increase of Christian persecution and oppression, we may not always have all the real estate and material trappings to which we are so accustomed. If we sincerely seek Him with all of our heart, He will be in our midst, whether we are worshiping at church, riding in an automobile, laboring at work, or engaging in some other activity.

We can continually seek His presence everywhere we go.

The laws of time and space do not confine God. He is omnipresent. Right this very moment, the Lord is with you, He is with me, and He is with every other person living on this earth. Isaiah prophesied that Jesus should be called *Emmanuel*, which means, "'God is with us'" (Isa. 7:14). He is not a supernatural being in Heaven who has no time for us lowly human beings. Jesus said, "'I am with you always, even to the end of the age'" (Matt. 28:20). Christ will not walk beside us today, only to abandon us tomorrow. He wants to dwell among us, continually helping us through the day-to-day challenges we face. He said, "'I have told you all this so that you may have peace in me. Here on earth you will have many trials and sorrows. But take heart, because I have overcome the world'" (John 16:33). Nothing will come as a surprise to Him, for He already has declared victory over every battle we encounter. He will be with us all of the days of our lives on this earth, and if we put our trust in Him, we will live in His presence forevermore (Ps. 23:6).

Worship does not begin with typing GPS coordinates into a tracking device, but with a focused heart set on worshiping God.

Jesus not only dwells among us, but He is also interceding on our behalf. Romans 8:34 says, "He is sitting in the place of honor at God's right hand, pleading for us." His love for us is so great that He not only gave His life on a cross for the forgiveness of our sins, but He continually makes intercession for us, knowing we will make mistakes, knowing we will need strength, and knowing we will need comfort. Jesus is a "friend who sticks closer than a brother" (Prov. 18:24 NIV). How many brothers would give their life for the sins of everyone on earth and then pray for the ones who had them crucified? This is a type of unconditional love seldom seen among mortal beings on this earth. First John 4:10 says, "This is real love—not that we loved God, but that he loved us and sent his Son as a sacrifice to take away our sins." God does not love us because we love Him. The reason He loves us is that God is the very embodiment of love (1 John 4:16).

The beautiful thing about the love of Christ is that God freely gives this abiding love to anyone who believes in Him. God does not reserve the gift of grace solely for wealthy executives, prominent celebrities, or even seemingly "good" people. This gift is for everyone who accepts Christ as Lord and Savior. When you confess your sins and call on the name of Jesus Christ, you can begin to develop a genuine relationship with the one true living God. As you grow in your walk with Christ, you will find you are never out of the reach of our Savior. Romans 8:39 says, "Nothing in all creation will ever be able to separate us from the love of God that is revealed in Christ Jesus our Lord." He will always be with us, for all eternity. Nothing on earth can separate us from His amazing, infinite love.

Conceivably, you may be perplexed, wondering how you can ever arrive at the place where the Lord is close enough to you that He is never more than an arm's reach away. The first step to knowing God personally is to seek Him with a sincere heart. James 4:8 (NIV) says, "Come near to God and he will come near to you." Being near to God is no secret. The Bible clearly states, if we draw close to God, then He will draw close to us. While we certainly should draw closer to Him continually, we must also realize that God is always near us. His presence is all around us. Even the psalmist David expressed the nearness of the Lord when he insightfully wrote, "I can never escape from your Spirit! I can never get away from your presence!" (Ps. 139:7). King David understood the omnipresence of Christ. He knew the Lord would walk with Him, even through the darkest valleys he encountered in life (Ps. 23:4). He knew the Lord would never leave him alone. He knew God would never fail.

Like King David, we need to trust the Lord wholeheartedly, realizing that our relationship with Jesus Christ is a two-way street. We must humbly come to Him, trusting His master plan for our lives. Jesus will never lead us astray. Deuteronomy 31:6 says, "He will neither fail you nor abandon you." He will always be standing, with arms open wide, waiting for us to accept His gift of everlasting love. He is not a god of broken promises. Nor is He a god of false compassion or a god of hierarchy. He humbled Himself when He came to earth. He struggled through life upon this earth, experiencing many of the hardships you and I encounter. Yet, He came not to complain over the shortcomings of this world; He came to redeem all humankind. He came to earth to be the God we have the opportunity to know on a personal level. He came to be our closest ally, our dearest friend, and our constant companion. He came to be "God with us."

Chapter Five

Worship Not Entertainment

"But everything that is done must strengthen all of you" (1 Cor. 14:26).

While many pastors and congregations claim to surrender fully to the leading of the Holy Spirit, their priorities and actions contradict their intention. From perfectly planned programs to succinctly scripted sermons, the objectives of these bodies of believers are well and good. Yet when it comes time for the service to begin, there is no room for the Holy Spirit to work in their midst. Not too long ago, I attended a church service where a few congregants seemed somewhat disgruntled because the segment of the service devoted to prayer requests and praise reports went on for nearly thirty minutes. Of course, this delay resulted in the service ending approximately twenty minutes after the noon hour. Upon seeing their reaction, I could not help but wonder at the likelihood of God's disappointment with the way His children react to certain situations within the house of the Lord.

Obviously, countless people attend church for social interaction more than they come to seek God. Rather than spend time duly in prayer, they would rather assemble over a cup of coffee and a pastry, hearing all of the local town gossip or catching up with their friends concerning a fabulous fishing trip or spectacular sporting event. While many people engross themselves in their own festivities and affairs, God is not looking for the next great event planner or social butterfly. He is looking for people who will worship Him in spirit and in truth. Jesus said, "'A time is coming and has now come when the true worshipers will worship the Father in the Spirit and in truth, for they are the kind of worshipers the Father seeks'" (John 4:23 NIV). This verse is not speaking of ancient biblical times, but it is speaking of the here and now. When we worship in spirit and in truth, God will seek us. He is seeking sincere worshipers this very moment.

Through the years, many different people have called, texted, or emailed me. Others have stopped me in the grocery store or visited my place of work. Some have even traveled to our home for food and fellowship after receiving an invitation from my family. While I appreciate all of the relatives, friends, and acquaintances whom God has blessed me with, there is no one I would rather hear from than my Father in Heaven. My primary purpose in life is to please the Lord in all I do. As Psalm 19:14 says, I pray the words of my mouth and the meditations of my heart will always be pleasing to the Lord. When I ponder the fact that God will seek me when I worship Him, my heart is overwhelmed with a special kind of joy that mere words cannot fully explain. I could not imagine refraining from worshiping my Lord and Savior, for nothing else satisfies my soul like praising His excellent name.

God is not looking for the next great event planner or social butterfly. He is looking for people who will worship Him in spirit and in truth.

I can only vaguely recall the first time I ever raised my hands in worship as a young child. Yet, even though I have worshiped the Lord countless times since, each time is special, like a precious gift bestowed upon me. The privilege of worshiping the One who loves me more than I could ever imagine holds a greater value than the rarest jewels a person could find. One of my most beloved experiences in life is to stand in a sanctuary filled with thousands of other Christians, calling on the name above every name, Jesus Christ. When we join our hearts in one accord, it seems as though God blesses us with a miniscule preview of what Heaven will be like.

In recent times, I was especially pleased when a friend sent me a message. She said she and her family would love to have the opportunity to worship with my dad and me when we visited her church. Her focus was not on increasing church membership nor was it centered on the possibility of all of us having the chance to catch up over dinner after the service. Instead, she understood the purpose of going to church. Psalm 26:8 says, "I love your sanctuary, LORD, the place where your glorious presence dwells." Notice this verse does not say the place where people socialize or the place where people go to fulfill their weekly duty. David wrote about the Lord's "glorious presence." How many churchgoers today would tell you they go to church because the Lord's presence dwells there? Although there would be some, I am afraid the numbers would be few.

When I enter the doors of a church sanctuary, I want the presence of the Lord to overwhelm me to the point where everything and everyone else around me takes a backseat to worshiping the Lord. Several months ago, I was standing near the front of a church sanctuary, waiting for the service to begin. Playing softly in the background was the song, "Psalm 23 (Surely Goodness, Surely Mercy)," written by Shane Barnard and Shane Everett. My mind was completely in tune with the lyrics of the song. I was so focused on the beautiful melody and inspiring message found within this song that I did not even notice a dear friend of ours walking up to me. Once they were directly in front of me, I finally noticed them. While it was a true pleasure to speak to them, I love the way I was not looking for people, but I was searching for God. How special it was to be so lost in His presence that I temporarily lost track of what was going on around me. Like King David, I love the place where God dwells. The joy and peace in my heart was so very great. All because I allowed the Holy Spirit to work in my heart and mind, and usher me into the sweet presence of the Almighty.

Worship is such an extraordinary part of my life, so I cannot truly grasp the reasons why some people would not want to commune with our Creator. God made us in His image (Gen. 1:27), yet some people have no desire even to talk to Him much less give Him glory, honor, and praise. It saddens my heart to know that many people miss such a tremendous blessing. Unfortunately, many churches are straying from worship the way it used to be. Even as a child, I can recall church services where the praise and worship music lasted far beyond a few hymns or choruses. Sometimes, the Holy Spirit would move in our midst, and praises to our Heavenly Father could continue to the end of the service. Now, the praise and worship segment of a service may range from nearly non-existent to something akin to a rock concert complete with elaborate lighting and fog machines. While many of the contemporary songs beautifully bring honor to God, there surely must be room for more than one era of worship music. It disappoints me when I visit churches where they no longer sing some of the familiar songs I grew up with, such as "Glory to His Name," "I Love You, Lord," and "What a Friend We Have in Jesus." Nevertheless, things are not as they used to be, considering the fact that true worship is often an afterthought in many church services today, and memorable melodies and theologically sound lyrics are being replaced by repetitious lyrics, generic melodies, and millennial whoops.

Even though his circumstances were different than my own, I echo the words of the psalmist David who wrote, "My heart is breaking as I remember how it used to be: I walked among the crowds of worshipers, leading a great procession to the house of God, singing for joy and giving thanks amid the sound of a great celebration!" (Ps. 42:4). The entire event known as "going to church" has drastically changed, even in the last couple of decades. Instead of church being seen as a way to renew one's spirit and sing praises to the King of kings and Lord of lords, it is now often considered a place to "do one's duty" by making a feeble effort to attend church. For some people, it makes them feel like a better person if they go to church. Others might be looking for a way to erase some guilt, and still others may attend church services simply to avoid sitting home alone for one hour per week. Whatever a person's reasons for attending church, it certainly seems as if reverence to God often falls pretty far down on the list.

For many people, worshiping God is more of a spectator sport. Other individuals believe worshiping God is about putting on airs for other people to see. It is disheartening to know that many people have the outward appearance of worshiping God, yet they do not actually worship Him in their heart. The Lord said, "'These people come near to me with their mouth and honor me with their lips, but their hearts are far from me'" (Isa. 29:13 NIV). Some people come to church with an enormous smile on their face, singing the praise songs proudly and raising their hands to the heavens. In reality, though, it is all for show. They want to *look* like a Christian. They want people to think they know how to worship, when they really have no concept of meaningful worship whatsoever. Their performance, if you will, is simply to draw attention to themselves as opposed to giving God the consideration He deserves. Worship must always be God-centered.

Jesus said, "'You must love the Lord your God with all your heart, all your soul, and all your mind'" (Matt. 22:37). Notice He did not say we should love the Lord our God a little bit or only with one piece of ourselves. We are to love the Lord with everything within us. God did not create us so we could split our praise between our favorite sports team, movie star, or recording artist, only reserving a small amount of praise for the Lord on Sundays. God created us so we could worship Him exclusively. If we love God with all of our heart, soul, and mind, then there will be nothing left over for other entities our earthly flesh may desire to honor. Rather than giving recognition to people, places, or things, which have no power to save us, we should give all of ourselves to God. He is the One who merits all of our praise.

Nonetheless, some people do not understand the importance of worshiping God. They feel worship is only something to check off the list once per week by going to church. Sadly, many people only darken the door of a church building on Christmas and Easter. These "holiday Christians" certainly fit the category of duty-led church attendance. The intricate decorations and frequently extravagant holiday pageants attract huge crowds largely because of their entertainment value. Of course, these individuals may just be living under the pretense of what a person *should* do, as opposed to anything they may actually want to do themselves. How disappointing it is to know that some people sitting in the pews on Sunday mornings literally have no clue about the meaning of it all. One pastor put the estimate at approximately sixty percent indifferent. Even sadder is the fact that some pastors are in the same predicament, leading a flock of congregants yet failing to realize why they are leading their congregation in the first place.

> *If we love God with all of our heart, soul, and mind, then there will be nothing left over for other entities our earthly flesh may desire to honor.*

In the midst of their confusion and frustration, many of them are leaving their churches at a rapid pace, with a large number of pastors departing the ministry every single month.

While these individuals are struggling to cope with the daily disappointments of life, they could take a lesson from God's creation. The psalmist David wrote about the way all creation proclaims the greatness of God on a daily basis in Psalm 19:1-4:

> The heavens proclaim the glory of God.
> The skies display his craftsmanship.
> Day after day they continue to speak;
> night after night they make him known.
> They speak without a sound or word;
> their voice is never heard.
> Yet their message has gone throughout the earth,
> and their words to all the world.

All day and all night long, God's marvelous creation makes His presence known. Unlike many people in the world today, they do not grow weary of bringing glory to the Creator. The birds do not get tired of flying and decide to take an extended break. The stars do not determine to turn themselves off, ceasing to light the night sky. The flowers and trees do not coordinate a protest against growing beautiful fragrant blooms and luscious fresh fruit. Not at all, for the sun, the moon, and all creation continuously displays His perfect majesty. Yet, in all of their radiance, the book of Psalms tells us, "Their voice is never heard." That is one thing that sets us apart from all of God's other unique creations. Men, women, boys, and girls are the only ones who can worship the Creator by speaking His name aloud. We have exclusive rights on worshiping God through words. We are the only ones who can declare His most holy name, sharing His amazing love with everyone we meet. It is up to you and I to proclaim the name above all names with a voice others can hear throughout the earth. God created us to worship the Lord in all we do, sharing the Gospel of Jesus Christ day after day, night after night.

Thankfully, there are devout Christians who continue to be witnesses for the Lord, always sharing the Gospel everywhere they go. Furthermore, there are churches, which serve as lighthouses within their communities. They have a common goal of reaching the lost, fulfilling the Great Commission as they share the Good News with everyone (Mark 16:15). One such church exists in the heart of downtown Brooklyn, serving as a godly refuge amid the hardened streets of New York City. God has blessed this ministry in a tremendous way, due to their sincere commitment to intercessory prayer and their focus on the One who matters most. Pastor Jim Cymbala often says the choir is singing to an audience of one, Jesus Christ. Everything they do is to give all glory to God, for He is the One who deserves all praise. They acknowledge the fact that a church service is not an entertainment venue, but a place for individuals from every tribe and tongue to magnify our Lord and Savior, Jesus Christ.

An Audience of One

> *"Then saith Jesus unto him, Get thee hence, Satan: for it is written, Thou shalt worship the Lord thy God, and him only shalt thou serve" (Matt. 4:10 KJV).*

Although the appearance of many church platforms would suggest otherwise, worship is not entertainment. When an individual stands on the platform at church, his or her goal should not be showing off their fashionable new clothes, flashing a beautiful smile at the camera, or even desiring people's applause. They should have one goal, and that is to point everyone in the congregation to Jesus Christ. Likewise, as congregants, we should not be gazing at the worship team or choir members, but focusing our eyes on Jesus. We are not there to sway to the music or impress the people around us; we are there to sing to an audience of one, Jesus Christ.

I fondly recall a video my dad and I once watched online of a remarkable organist in California by the name of Derrick Jackson. He played a marvelous medley of gospel songs with expert accuracy and musical interpretation. At the end, the congregation who had been worshiping the Lord, stood and enthusiastically applauded his efforts. Rather than accept the praise given to him, he did something more surprising and profound than his skilled musicianship. He turned his back to the congregants, folded his hands, and humbly gave God all of the glory. He understood that his place was not to entertain the people, but to exalt the Lord.

A church service is not an entertainment venue, but a place for individuals from every tribe and tongue to magnify our Lord and Savior, Jesus Christ.

In the fall of 2019, my dad and I had the opportunity to attend The Brooklyn Tabernacle Music Conference. Phil Wickham was the guest artist for this special event. After he led the conference attendees in a selection of praise and worship songs, he began leading everyone in singing the beloved hymn, "How Great Thou Art." In the middle of the song, he did something very few musical recording artists would even consider. He put his guitar down and walked off the platform. He did not stay for applause, nor did he seek recognition of any kind. He simply walked off stage quietly as all twelve hundred voices joined in harmony, lifting praises to the King of kings and Lord of lords. Instead of making worship about Phil Wickham, he made worship about Jesus Christ. This example is one we should all strive to follow. Worshiping the Lord is not about having impressive stage presence; worshiping the Lord is about glorifying the wonderful name of Jesus Christ with everything that is within us.

> *Worshiping the Lord is not about having impressive stage presence; worshiping the Lord is about glorifying the wonderful name of Jesus Christ with everything that is within us.*

In my inspirational autobiography, *When You're in the Sunset, There's Sunshine Awaiting You*, I shared the story of a gentleman my dad and I had the privilege of hearing sing in the Great Smoky Mountains. I pray my account of this touching example of someone who wholeheartedly worshiped the Lord in spirit and in truth will bless you.

Several years ago, my dad and I visited a church in Cherokee, North Carolina. During the service, one of the members of the congregation sang a special song. This elderly gentleman poured his heart into every single note. Although it may not have been a performance deemed "good enough" to grace many prominent stages in the world, it was something I will always remember. The zeal and love for our Lord that he expressed through this single song embodied a greater message than a month of sermons could convey. His aim was not to please the congregation, but to please his Lord and Savior, Jesus Christ. As he sang, he held nothing back. He passionately sang of his anticipation of seeing Christ. He gave everything he could to the delivery of this song, so that it might be pleasing to our Heavenly Father. Through his ministry, I know God used him to touch people's hearts. How do I know? I know because his song touched my own heart in a special way.[1]

To this very day, I can clearly recall the goose bumps that covered my arms as this Native American man humbly delivered this song of praise to the Lord. Affectionately known as Brother Squirrel, he could certainly teach all of us about what it really means to worship. He was not concerned with the congregation or what they thought about how he sang. He was in tune with Jesus Christ throughout the entire song, giving all of the glory to the One who is most deserving of all praise. Brother Squirrel unreservedly knew the purpose of worship. Worship is not about pleasing people; worship is about pleasing God.

Having perfect pitch will not earn you salvation. Playing an innovative rendition of a beautiful song will not save you. Preaching a well-written sermon will not get you into Heaven. If you are living your life strictly to provide entertainment or to enjoy amusement of some kind, then you are not fulfilling God's purpose for your life. My dad wrote, "Unfortunately, many preachers and pastors focus too much attention on comedy, storytelling, and showmanship."[2] God did not create us for entertainment. He created us to proclaim His praise (Isa. 43:21). We are not on this earth to extol one another, nor are we here to bring attention to ourselves. Our Creator purposefully designed us to give Him glory. Our lives should be a living testimony of His grace and mercy, whether we are sitting with a few of our colleagues at our workplace, catching up with dozens of relatives at a family reunion, or standing in front of hundreds or even thousands of congregants in church. Everything we do should bring honor to God.

When we stand on the platform at church or any other location on this planet, we have an important reputation to uphold. It is far more than our personal reputations, for we are the ones representing the King of kings and Lord of lords. Second Corinthians 5:20 says, "We are Christ's ambassadors; God is making his appeal through us." Our mission in life should be to shine forth the love of Christ everywhere we go. Consider this: what if your employer asked you to give a presentation at a prominent business meeting, which would influence the direction the company would take for the next five or ten years? Surely, you would make careful preparation, doing all you could to ensure you upheld the company's image. By comparison, we should diligently labor to ensure our lives demonstrate the love of Jesus Christ every day of our lives. Sharing His love with people whom God places in our paths could be the determining factor in whether they choose to accept Jesus Christ as their Lord and Savior. If we put ourselves before Christ, we could be the one thing standing between them and the Lord. As opposed to having a five or ten-year impact on a corporation, each time we speak to other people has the potential to influence their life for eternity.

Nevertheless, some people seem to gloss over this vital truth, acting as if nothing they do could possibly have an effect on another person. To complicate matters further, they live as if they are on this earth for the sole purpose of making themselves happy. Rather than give their lives to serving others, or most importantly, serving the Lord, they focus on themselves, neglecting the notion that their testimony of God's faithfulness in their life could save someone on the verge of suicide. Recently, someone emailed me and said they thought ending their life would make them feel okay. They did not contact me so they could hear the latest weather report or even to hear my life story. Nor did they reach out to me, hoping I would simply tell them to go and live their best life. They emailed me because they needed encouragement from the Word of God, reassuring them that there is hope beyond their circumstances. They needed someone to tell them that God created them for a purpose, reaffirming the fact their life is valuable. They needed someone to remind them that Jesus Christ loves them more than they could ever begin to imagine.

I will always remember our visit to Nanortalik, a small fishing village in southern Greenland. With a population of less than twelve hundred, Nanortalik Church singlehandedly serves the spiritual needs of the entire community. As we walked through the doors of this historic church built in 1916, a small group of native Greenlanders was singing hymns of praise to God. After the concert, we gave them some Gospel tracts we had written to encourage them. My dad also had the opportunity to play their organ, which featured hand-carved wooden keys. The chance to encourage these fellow believers was truly special. We spoke to many people throughout the town as well. Seeing the downcast faces of young and old was heartbreaking. Although a small number in this remote area serve the Lord, the lack of adequate sunlight during the year coupled with the struggling economy causes many people to succumb to depression and alcoholism. Greenland's suicide rate is reportedly among the highest in the world. The people living in this region do not need someone to entertain them or to offer a five-step program designed to help them achieve success. They need the eternal hope that only comes from knowing Jesus Christ.

People do not need a parade of motivational speakers or flashy entertainers. There are already plenty of those in the secular world. Even so, many churches spend millions of dollars, striving to provide a family-friendly entertainment venue as opposed to a beacon of hope to a lost and dying world. Not too long ago, someone told me of a visit to a friend's church near Atlanta, Georgia. As they summarized their experience, all they said was that there were many lights on the platform and loud music. Yet, this worldly display did not intrigue them a bit, despite the fact they are a member of the younger generation and a previous member of a rock band. Instead, they were disappointed to find such goings-on within the church. They had nothing to say regarding the pastor's sermon. There were no comments made concerning the messages conveyed through the lyrics of the songs sung. They went to church, watched a show, and returned home. The whole purpose of assembling for a church service was lost in translation due to this church's desire to be *like* the world instead of being a *light* to the world. As my dad said, "Boats are put in water. That is their purpose. However, if water gets in the boat, it will sink. The church should be in the world; the world should not be in the church."

When individuals walk into a church sanctuary, they need to find spiritual refreshment. The worship team and musicians should be leading people into a spirit of worship, not doing all they can to provide the latest beat with which people can mindlessly clap their hands. Likewise, the purpose of the pastor is not to entertain their congregants. It is not the minister's job to serve as the Sunday morning comedian, or motivational speaker, but to serve as the shepherd of their flock. The apostle Paul summarized the purpose of a worship service when he wrote, "Let everything be constructive *and* edifying *and* done for the good of all the church" (1 Cor. 14:26 AMP). When we gather to worship our Lord and Savior, Jesus Christ, we should have two goals. One should be to glorify the King of kings and Lord of lords. Our second goal

The church should be in the world; the world should not be in the church.

should be to provide spiritual strength to our brothers and sisters in Christ. If congregants do not leave the church sanctuary feeling revived spiritually, ready to confidently battle through another week, then the church has completely failed. As the apostle Paul wrote, "everything," meaning the music, the sermon, the prayer time, and all that is in-between, must serve to strengthen everyone.

Church should always be spiritually edifying to everyone in the congregation. The

Church should be a conduit of encouragement, not a means of entertainment.

intention of praise and worship music is not to provide young people with the opportunity to dance. Preachers should not deliver sermons in an effort to give people in the congregation a sense of self-proclaimed empowerment or attempt to get people excited by shouting at the top of their lungs. Children's ministry programs do not exist to provide a free babysitting service for parents and guardians one or two hours per week. Even the nursery should not be a place for aimless playtime or naptime, for the Bible says children should be brought "up in the training and instruction of the Lord" (Eph. 6:4 NIV). Although this instruction should originate at home, the church should reinforce the godly principles children learn from their parents. Activities for young adults, senior citizens, widows, and other specialized groups should all serve to edify the saints. Church should be a conduit of encouragement, not a means of entertainment.

Pastors and other church leaders need to remember that the people who enter the sanctuary doors are battling the same trials they themselves encounter each week. Mothers and fathers enter church services emotionally and physically drained from the busy events of the week. Children and teens face all manner of negative influences throughout the week, coming from other people, the television, the Internet, and many other sources. Single adults could be wondering if they will ever find a spouse or be alone for the rest of their lives. Other adults may be seeking God's purpose for their lives following retirement, or they may be trying to adjust to an empty nest. Some people may be struggling with drug addiction, depression, or suicidal thoughts. Everyone has a story. We all encounter difficulties every single day. As such, the church should serve as a triage center, providing aid for the diverse needs of the congregation. People need to know that someone cares, that someone loves them, and that they are not alone. As James 1:27 says, this is part of our worship and pure religion.

Jesus Christ is the only One who deserves the spotlight.

This Sunday morning, someone sitting in the pew in front of you could be going through a dreadfully dark valley, needing a shoulder to lean on or maybe even to cry on. Perhaps they just received a cancer diagnosis, where the doctor told them they only have a few months to live. Rather than considering their own health concerns, they could be troubled over the fear of leaving behind their spouse and children. An entertaining sermon or foot-tapping song is not going to help them all that much, no more than a conversation about current events is truly going to lift their spirits. They need a dose of divine inspiration, which can only come from God. This individual needs fellow churchgoers to go to the throne of grace, praying on their behalf, while reminding them that the Lord heals all of our diseases (Ps. 103:3). Like the person facing a battle with cancer, countless individuals are experiencing equally distressing situations, anxiously searching for true, lasting hope. We need to be the ones to tell them that Jesus Christ is the only source of eternal hope. The church should be a lighthouse to the community and to the world, careful to focus on delivering spiritual encouragement not secular entertainment, for Jesus Christ is the only One who deserves the spotlight. He alone deserves all of our praise.

Chapter Six

The Power of Praise

"'The LORD is my strength and my song; he has given me victory. This is my God, and I will praise him—my father's God, and I will exalt him!'" (Exod. 15:2).

*A*s someone who holds a Master of Science degree in English Education, I fully appreciate the importance of effective verbal and written communication. In fact, it seems God has given me an astute eye for detail when it comes to finding spelling and grammar errors in all sorts of written compositions. People who know me will likely chuckle when I mention that I even have a tendency to proofread everything from road signs to cereal boxes. Without giving it so much as a thought, I constantly point out capitalization and punctuation errors, even within professional publications. While I am somewhat guilty of being a card-carrying member of the "grammar police," I fondly recall a time when perfectly proofread prose was the furthest thing from my mind, for I had no concern as to whether or not the letters had all flawlessly fallen into place in my mind.

In 2018, my dad and I returned to Eastern Europe. Our first stop was Bucharest, Romania, where I sang and shared my testimony at a women's conference on Friday evening. What a special blessing to be able to encourage these ladies and to share a special time of prayer with them. We spent all day Saturday evangelizing with the pastor within the local community, praying for people on the street and sharing the Gospel with them. On Sunday, we had the joy of ministering in word and song at Hope

Baptist Church and Spiritual Revival Baptist Church. As the morning service began, I was awestruck by the opportunity to stand inside this beautiful sanctuary, singing praises to Jesus Christ. Although I have worshiped Him continually since my childhood, this experience was truly extra special. The congregants jubilantly sang the lyrics in their native tongue. As I clumsily stumbled over the pronunciation of the Romanian words appearing on the screen, I found the Spirit of the Lord transcended all language barriers in existence. The message was loud and clear. Everyone knew the One who deserved our praise. Our hearts were worshiping together in one accord, and the Holy Spirit stirred our hearts in a life-changing manner.

It is hard to put into words just how extraordinary it was to witness this spiritual harmony in the midst of verbal discord. Reflecting back on this unique occasion, I feel as if I had a miniscule taste of what the believers experienced in Jerusalem on the Day of Pentecost. Of course, language was no longer a communicative obstacle when the Holy Spirit came upon them. Acts 2:2-4 says, "Suddenly, there was a sound from heaven like the roaring of a mighty windstorm, and it filled the house where they were sitting. Then, what looked like flames or tongues of fire appeared and settled on each of them. And everyone present was filled with the Holy Spirit and began speaking in other languages, as the Holy Spirit gave them this ability." Because of the power of the Holy Spirit, everyone in the room was able to speak languages other than their own. Before you jump to conclusions, these individuals had not spent countless years studying foreign languages in a prominent educational institution. God's Word says, "The Holy Spirit gave them this ability" (Acts 2:4). Through the power of God, they had new language skills, so they would be able to communicate with the people outside.

As soon as people on the city streets below began to hear their own languages spoken, they instantly took notice. When God moves, He often moves in a mighty way. Jewish people from many different nations "came running, and they were bewildered to hear their own languages being spoken by the believers" (Acts 2:6). The Bible says these people from other diverse ethnic groups "were completely amazed" (Acts 2:7). In fact, they all questioned how this was even possible. They said, "'These people are all from Galilee, and yet we hear them speaking in our own native languages'" (Acts 2:7-8). What many of the Jewish people failed to realize then was that God was the One who gave the believers the ability to speak in other languages, so they would also have the opportunity to hear "about the wonderful things God has done" (Acts 2:11). God knew the power of the Holy Spirit moving in their midst would not only encourage the believers, but would also serve as a witness to others.

Without the Holy Spirit, true worship cannot take place.

While we may never personally witness such a miracle as occurred among the 120 believers that day, we can be certain God will work in our midst when we join together to honor our Lord. The believers in the book of Acts experienced the power of the Holy Spirit as they gathered together (Acts 2:1). Their primary purpose for assembling was to praise God and lift up His holy name. Jesus said, "'Where two or three gather in my name, there am I with them'" (Matt. 18:20 NIV). As these believers came together, Jesus was in their midst. God honored their worship by sending the Holy Spirit to anoint them. Without the Holy Spirit, true worship cannot take place. Because their worship ushered in the Spirit of the living God, lives were eternally changed. Even though some people mocked them and suggested they were drunk on wine, their act of obedience to God was not in vain

(Acts 2:13). The apostle Peter shared the Gospel message, pleading with the Jews to call on the name of the Lord. Approximately three thousand people accepted the gift of salvation through Christ that very day (Acts 2:41).

What an amazing testimony of the power of worship. If these early Christians had not joined in worship that day, perhaps those three thousand souls would have forever been lost. Because these believers obeyed the leading of the Holy Spirit, eternal change took hold within the heart of these once lost individuals. What would happen today if God called a large group of people together for a time of worship? I am not talking about a regularly scheduled church service on Sunday, or even a mid-week prayer meeting, but a divine appointment not yet written on the calendar or stored in a digital device. Sadly, people today might be hard-pressed to find time to fit one more thing into their busy schedule, even if it was an encounter with the Holy Spirit. Unfortunately, many people have not yet come to the realization that we need God now just as much as our ancestors did.

First Peter 5:8 (NIV) says, "Your enemy the devil prowls around like a roaring lion looking for someone to devour." Satan wants to destroy every person on earth, Christians and non-Christians alike. He desires to possess every soul, leading them down the path that leads to eternal destruction. Yet, Jesus said, "'Enter through the narrow gate. For wide is the gate and broad is the road that leads to destruction, and many enter through it. But small is the gate and narrow the road that leads to life, and only a few find it'" (Matt. 7:13-14 NIV). Regardless of the pressures life may place upon us, we cannot succumb to the devil's schemes. We must plant our feet on the narrow path, determined to follow the Lord's steps every day of our lives. More than that, we need to "put on the full armor of God," so we can stand against whatever Satan plots against us (Eph. 6:11 NIV). God's Word says, "For our struggle is not against flesh and blood, but against the rulers, against the authorities, against the powers of this dark world and against the spiritual forces of evil in the heavenly realms. Therefore put on the full armor of God, so that when the day of evil comes, you may be able to stand your ground, and after you have done everything, to stand" (Eph. 6:12-13 NIV). The only way we can prevail against the wickedness of this world is if we stand firm on the solid Rock, Jesus Christ. Without the presence of God, there is no protection.

Perhaps you are wondering how you can be sure to have the presence of the Lord in your life. You may think you are not good enough to warrant a visit from the Holy Spirit like the believers on the Day of Pentecost. You will be happy to know that you are in large company, for no single person on this planet is *good enough*. Romans 3:23 says, "For everyone has sinned; we all fall short of God's glorious standard." We have all made mistakes. We have all intentionally committed sins. Even though none of us are worthy on our own to receive such a tremendous gift, God extends His amazing grace to all who will believe. He has provided a way for us to receive the gift of eternal life. If we want the Lord to be present in our daily lives, we must call on His name. The Lord said He would always answer us when we call on Him (Jer. 33:3). He wants to help us throughout our lives, but we have to be willing to humble ourselves and ask Him for help. When we surrender our hearts to Him, then God will reveal His glory in ways we could never even begin to imagine.

Praise Leads to Victory

"But thanks be to God, who always leads us in triumph in Christ" (2 Cor. 2:14 AMP).

Even King Jehoshaphat realized his need for the Lord's protection against the armies of the Moabites, Ammonites, and

Meunites. He may have been the ruler of the entire kingdom of Judah, but Jehoshaphat knew he could not make it on his own. He knew they could never defeat these armies without the Lord on their side. As such, he pleaded with the Lord for His help. Jehoshaphat prayed, "'O our God, won't you stop them? We are powerless against this mighty army that is about to attack us. We do not know what to do, but we are looking to you for help'" (2 Chron. 20:12). King Jehoshaphat did not try to flaunt his power. Instead of arrogantly talking about being king, he humbly cried out to the King of kings. Jehoshaphat openly said they were powerless against the fierce soldiers who were closing in on them. Without God's help, he knew they could all lose their lives at the hands of the enemy.

Nonetheless, the key to victory was not simply a prayer of desperation. As they were standing together in prayer, the Spirit of the Lord came upon a man named Jahaziel. He said, "'Listen, all you people of Judah and Jerusalem! Listen, King Jehoshaphat! This is what the LORD says: Do not be afraid! Don't be discouraged by this mighty army, for the battle is not yours, but God's'" (2 Chron. 20:15). Then, Jahaziel spoke these reassuring words: "'But you will not even need to fight. Take your positions; then stand still and watch the LORD's victory'" (2 Chron. 20:17). Through the power of the Holy Spirit, God used Jahaziel to deliver a message to King Jehoshaphat and the constituents in his kingdom. They called; God answered. However, the real miracle occurred the morning after they bowed down to worship the Lord God Almighty.

In modern times, most generals going into battle would command the ordnance unit to distribute appropriate weaponry to the soldiers positioned on the front line. King Jehoshaphat, however, took a much different approach. Second Chronicles 20:21 says, "After consulting the people, the king appointed singers to walk ahead of the army, singing to the LORD and praising him for his holy splendor. This is what they sang: 'Give thanks to the Lord; his faithful love endures forever!'" Just imagine! A massive army was approaching them, and he decided to replace the most advanced tactical combat units with a vocal ensemble. While this unconventional warfare strategy may sound somewhat illogical, the hand of the Almighty guided King Jehoshaphat. The king knew God would not fail them. He knew God would keep His promise. He knew they only needed to "'stand still and watch the LORD's victory,'" just as they had been instructed by the Holy Spirit (2 Chron. 20:17).

Although many things transpired before this critical battle, the most important action on the part of the king and the people around him was their obedience to God. They prayed, and they praised. When they praised the Lord, God intervened. According to God's Word, "At the very moment they began to sing and give praise, the LORD caused the armies of Ammon, Moab, and Mount Seir to start fighting among themselves" (2 Chron. 20:22). Instead of fighting their enemies, these allied forces attacked one another. When King Jehoshaphat's army reached "the lookout point in the wilderness, all they saw were dead bodies lying on the ground as far as they could see. Not a single one of the enemy had escaped" (2 Chron. 20:24). God spared the king and the army of Judah because they followed the Lord's leading. When they praised God through song, they immediately experienced the power of worship.

When they lifted their voices in song, notice they did not sing a song of defeat. Instead, they sang a song of thanksgiving and praise to the Lord. They glorified the Lord through their worship, even in the midst of an alarming situation. They did not give in to the hopelessness they might have felt, nor did they sit down and cry. Through the power of God, they had the courage to trust the Lord completely. Rather than rely on a standard battleground approach, they chose to stand on Holy Ground by ushering in the presence of the Lord through songs of worship.

When we open our hearts to the Lord and worship Him in

one accord, the Spirit of God will move. In order to see the Lord at work in our lives, we have to come to the solid conclusion that God is the One who deserves all of the credit. He is the only One to whom we should give honor. Unfortunately, many people believe they are the ones who are the sole reason something good happens in their lives. There are even pastors and evangelists who direct praise to themselves, their deacons, their worship team, or others in the church. While it may seem that these individuals are irreplaceable when it comes to running a ministerial organization, giving direct praise to another person is not going to result in a powerful move of God.

The only type of praise that will lead to victorious ends is the uninhibited praises sounding forth to honor the only true living God. God's Word says the Lord inhabits the praises of His people (Ps. 22:3). When we praise God, He hears us. He enters into our hearts, our souls, and our minds through the Holy Spirit. If we come to Him with a mindset of sincere worship, then He will not only bless our lives, but He will fill us with His unprecedented peace. Philippians 4:6-7 (NIV) says, "Do not be anxious about anything, but in every situation, by prayer and petition, with thanksgiving, present your requests to God. And the peace of God, which transcends all understanding, will guard your hearts and your minds in Christ Jesus." Although this passage contains wonderful promises from God's Word, I would contend that the two most important words in this passage are simply, "with thanksgiving." We can pray about a situation in our

> *The only type of praise that will lead to victorious ends is the uninhibited praises sounding forth to honor the only true living God.*

lives all day and all night, but if we are not thankful to God, then we may not receive this true incomprehensible peace. This verse says we need to come to the throne of grace with a grateful heart. Our thankfulness to God should extend beyond the church sanctuary, into our everyday existence.

While there are many ways to offer thanks to God, I frequently find myself singing songs of praise as I go about my daily activities. Even as I am washing dishes, checking email, or walking through the grocery store, my mind often wanders away from the cares of this world as I quietly hum tunes like, "My Tribute (To God Be the Glory)," "You Are Holy," "I Sing Praises," or another song written to magnify the matchless name of Jesus. I have fond memories of going to church as a child, singing praise and worship songs, such as, "Give Thanks" and "Thank You, Lord (For Saving My Soul)." Thankfully, some things never change, for I still love singing songs of thanksgiving to our Lord and Savior. While it may be easy for us to thank God for His many blessings as we sing songs of praise on a beautiful Sunday morning when all is well in our little world, it becomes an uphill battle when we attempt to thank Him during a difficult trial in our lives. Worshiping the Lord is easier standing in a church sanctuary than it is standing in a hospital room or a funeral home. Although there will be moments in life when it will seem nearly impossible to utter a word of praise to God, these are the times when we need to praise Him even more.

Our thankfulness to God should extend beyond the church sanctuary, into our everyday existence.

On August 2, 2008, my precious mama went home to be with the Lord. My parents and I were on vacation in the midst of the picturesque Great Smoky Mountains in North Carolina. One moment, everything seemed perfect. The next moment, life seemingly spiraled out of control. My mom had a heart attack. As I called 911, my mind was racing. I cried out to God for His mercy. I could not understand why He did not intervene. My heart was broken into a million pieces. In that moment of complete and utter despair, praising God seemed the furthest thing from my mind. As we sat down beside my mother's earthen vessel, though, my dad and I sang the song, "Living by Faith." Although my mind could not begin to comprehend the tragic circumstances surrounding us, I worshiped the Lord from the depths of my soul.

Looking back, I do not know how I would have made it through this dark valley on my own, even with my dad's constant love and support. Many people often quote the old adage, "Time heals all wounds." I beg to differ. God is the One who heals all wounds. He is the One who brought my dad and me through this heartbreaking tragedy in our lives. Through much heartfelt prayer and praise, sometimes through streams of tears, God restored my joy. It was nothing I did on my own. I give all of the glory and praise to Him for allowing my dad and me to find a new normal, a new routine, and a new purpose for our lives, now that my sweet mama is worshiping at the feet of Jesus Christ.

You could be inquiring, how can you praise the Lord when He did not spare your mother? My question to you would be how could I afford *not* to praise His precious holy name? How could I be ungrateful for all of His wondrous blessings, including the cherished years I had with my incredible mom? How could I cease worshiping the One who gave me life when I was born premature without a heartbeat? How could I stop loving the One who loved me so much that He gave His life for me? Even through the many trials and tribulations that I have experienced in my life, I can say with complete assurance that I have never lost my faith in God. He has always proven faithful to me. Just as

His Word promises, God fills my heart and mind with peace beyond all understanding when I come to Him with thanksgiving (Phil. 4:6-7). I will never stop giving thanks to Him, for I have made the life-changing choice to worship Him for all eternity.

In 2014, I wrote a song titled, "Thank You, Lord." The lyrics carry a special meaning for me, as they are more than just words I sing. They are a deeply sincere proclamation of my heart. No matter what is going on around me, I can always thank the Lord for His love, His mercy, and His grace. I am truly grateful for the gift of this song, as I know the Holy Spirit is the One who gave me these special words, declaring the Lord's majesty.

> The colors of the sunset,
> The twinkling of the stars,
> The glory of each sunrise,
> And the mountains from afar;
> From the onset of creation,
> You have shown Your majesty.
> But the greatest gift You've given,
> You gave at Calvary.
>
> I know sometimes I question
> The plan You have for me.
> But every time I've failed You,
> You've loved me patiently.
> Lord, You know what's best;
> In You, I find sweet rest.
> So I trust in You alone,
> And I bow before Your throne.
>
> *Chorus:*
> Thank You, Lord,
> For Your boundless love.
> Thank You, Lord,

For everything You've done.
I raise my hands in worship;
You're the One whom I adore.
Standing humbly in Your presence,
I praise and thank You, Lord.

I am always in Your presence.
I praise and thank You, Lord.[1]

Thanking the Lord for His love and His mercy is something we should do every day. He deserves our wholehearted gratitude for everything He does for us. Still, we must never lose sight of the fact that our greatest form of worship is not praising Him for His abundant blessings or giving thanks for the spiritual fulfillment we gain from being in His presence. Real worship can only occur when we humble ourselves before the Lord in complete surrender. Watchman Nee said, "Those who do not stop at God's gifts but who also seek His face are those who can truly worship. One who is not surrendered to God cannot worship."[2] Rather than look to God for things, we must give our all as we worship Him for the solitary fact that He is God. This is true worship.

Still, many people fail to realize the purpose of worship. Likewise, they disregard the sovereignty of God. In a world of imperfection, disappointment, and discouragement, it becomes very easy for us to question God. We wonder why He allows bad things to happen. We may feel as if He has abandoned us. Yet, the entire time we are waywardly searching for answers, the answer is right in front of us. God is always with us. He is the answer for every problem we face. Even when we doubt Him, He is standing with open arms, waiting patiently for us to come running to Him. We must place our trust in Him completely. When we bow before Him, humbling ourselves and surrendering to His perfect will, then we will find sweet rest for our souls. He will surround us with His radiant peace that extends beyond any form of peace this world could offer. Through His unwavering compassion, He will remind us of our need for His presence in our lives. When we genuinely accept the fact that our Father truly knows best, then we can have the calm assurance that the same God who created the sunrises and sunsets, as well as the twinkling stars and distant mountains, is the same One who created you and me. His glory will astound us anew, renewing our desire to worship Him with thanksgiving.

Giving thanks to the Lord is a form of worship. When we joyfully proclaim, "Thank You, Lord," or sing another song of thanksgiving, we are giving glory to the Lord for His help, His companionship, and His love, which has no bounds. He is the One who deserves all of our adoration. We should take every opportunity to raise our hands, worshiping His holy

Rather than look to God for things, we must give our all as we worship Him for the solitary fact that He is God. This is true worship.

name. We should thank the Lord constantly, for we will never be able to thank Him enough for His divine presence in our lives. Likewise, we should not only praise Him for His many blessings, but we should honor Him for who He is. He is the King of kings and Lord of lords. He is our "Wonderful Counselor, Mighty God, Everlasting Father, [and] Prince of Peace" (Isa. 9:6 NIV). He is worthy of all of our praise, simply because He is God. We should never stop humbling ourselves before our Heavenly Father and giving thanks to Him.

First Thessalonians 5:18 (NIV) says we should "give thanks in all circumstances." Giving thanks in all circumstances does not

mean we need to start thanking God for a flat tire, a lost job, or a lengthy illness. However, it does mean we should thank God in the midst of these or any other unsettling situations. By failing to praise Him, we forfeit the treasured opportunity to commune with our Creator. As Psalm 22:3 says, the Lord inhabits the praises of His people. We need the Lord every day, but surely we need the Lord to be with us in the midst of our trials most of all. Therefore, we must make a concerted effort to thank the Lord, in the sunshine and the rain. When we do, we will find that the nearness of His presence will soothe our sorrow and restore our joy. He will give us everlasting hope beyond anything this world could ever offer.

> *Praise the Lord for what He has done and for what He will do. Above all, praise Him for who He is.*

Until we can let go of our anxiety, we will likely never experience true, unhindered worship. The worries of life metaphorically serve as unnecessary baggage we carry around with us. When our hands are full of this figurative baggage, raising our hands in worship could be a struggle. When we grow weary from hauling these things around all day, it will likely be difficult to have clarity of mind when we spend time in God's Word. When we stress over the cares of this life, we may miss God's gift of peace because we disregard the fact that God has everything under control. We must let go of our sorrowfulness, our fretful nature, and our disheartening circumstances, giving all of our cares to the Lord, for He cares for us (1 Pet. 5:7).

God wants to help us through every bump in the road. Nothing will come as a surprise to Him, for He is the One who has mapped out a master plan for each of our lives. Yet, He gives us the choice of either attempting to clear the obstacles on our own or coming to Him for strength. As I can tell you from personal experience, it will always be easier to climb monumental mountains and forge raging rivers with God on your side. Lay your burdens down at the altar and trust our Heavenly Father. Praise the Lord for what He has done and for what He will do. Above all, praise Him for who He is. When you praise the name of Jesus Christ, He will transform your defeat into victory!

Chapter Seven

Worship Replaces Worry

"Don't worry about anything; instead, pray about everything. Tell God what you need, and thank him for all he has done. Then you will experience God's peace, which exceeds anything we can understand. His peace will guard your hearts and minds as you live in Christ Jesus" (Phil. 4:6-7).

*I*n the fall of 2018, I experienced one of the most difficult trials of my life. A severe throbbing in my right leg escalated into a three-month long battle, which threatened my life. Many days, I would sit on our sofa at home with tears rolling down my cheeks because of the intensity of the pain. The symptoms caused critical side effects, including dangerously high blood pressure. Following multiple scans, tests, and appointments, the doctors presented some discouraging images to my dad and me on September 28, 2018. The MRI results showed what looked like a mass, which had grown to the entire width of my leg. As I heard the physicians saying words like *cancer, oncology,* and *amputation,* my mind raced with the implications of the possible diagnoses. My dad and I found this news to be greatly discouraging. I remember crying myself to sleep that night with long, deep sobs, wondering what the coming days would bring.

Even in the midst of these dismal circumstances, I had peace beyond all human understanding. My dad and I held on to the promise in God's Word that says we can receive healing through the stripes Jesus bore on the cross (Isa. 53:5). We knew God would walk beside us in the midst of this horrible trial. In

October, I had surgery to repair damaged arteries in my leg, caused by my connective tissue disorder. God healed me, and mercifully allowed me to avoid cancer and to keep my leg as well. I give Him all of the glory, honor, and praise. Despite what some of the medical experts were telling me, I knew God would never fail. I thank God for the caring specialist who patiently operated on my leg for three tedious hours. The right doctor at the right time is sometimes very critical. Then and now, I believe God made the arrangements, and His hand was at work. I had calm assurance that He would give me peace in the middle of this dark valley.

Philippians 4:6-7 says, "Don't worry about anything; instead, pray about everything. Tell God what you need, and thank him for all he has done. Then you will experience God's peace, which exceeds anything we can understand. His peace will guard your hearts and minds as you live in Christ Jesus." This passage in God's Word is not referring to the eternal peace we will one day have in Heaven, for we will not experience anxiety when we are forever at home with the Lord. I do not believe anyone in Heaven will be standing around the throne of God asking for peace, as peace will certainly abound when we are in the presence of the King of kings and Lord of lords.

On the contrary, life on this earth is a continuous stream of tribulations and trials, so our unending need for peace is truly great. Philippians chapter four tells us how to have peace even in the most violent storms of life. First, we must pray. However, we cannot simply present our requests to God. We must also come before Him with thanksgiving. We must be thankful. You may be wondering how you are supposed to be grateful for a calamity that comes your way. God is not demanding that we thank Him *for* the trials, but instead, we are to thank Him and praise Him in the *midst* of the trials.

When we pray and thank Him for everything He has done, then we will receive God's perfect peace. Someone may experience peace as they relax beside a resort-style pool, walk along the sandy shores of the ocean, or hike through the lofty peaks of a towering mountain range, but the peace spoken of in this scripture is something which cannot be discovered on this earth without the intervention of the hand of the Almighty. The Bible clearly tells us this peace exceeds our own human knowledge (Phil. 4:7). Therefore, we will never be able to explain this peace nor can we ever fully understand the way it helps us make it through difficult situations in life. What we can know for sure, though, is that this unprecedented peace is an essential element to enduring the hardships life brings our way. Without the peace of God, we will be like an out of control ship hazardously drifting into an outcropping of jagged rocks. Unless we have His hedge of protection, we will have no hope for the future. He is our only source of true peace.

God is not demanding that we thank Him for the trials, but instead, we are to thank Him and praise Him in the midst of the trials.

Although we know God will grant us peace, there are moments in life when we may find it difficult to have the words to speak. Perhaps we become troubled to the point where we can no longer utter a prayer request or a word of thanksgiving, simply because we cannot muster up the strength to do so. As I endured such a physical battle in 2018, there were times when the pain in my leg was so great that I could barely even speak. I had confidence the Lord would bring me through, but sometimes, I felt as if this trial was seemingly without end. I felt like the psalmist David who questioned the Lord, inquiring, "How long, LORD?" (Ps. 13:1

NIV). He wondered if God had completely forgotten him. He went on to ask, "How long must I wrestle with my thoughts and day after day have sorrow in my heart?" (Ps. 13:2 NIV). He was terribly worried and distraught, much as I was when I was facing such life-threatening health concerns. It seemed my dad and I prayed diligently, yet no answers came. Day after day, week after week, month after month, I sought the Lord for comfort, healing, and deliverance.

When we feel as if we are nearing the last thread of hope, we need to remember who created the threads of our lives in the first place.

Is this you? Are you seeking an answer from God today? Perhaps you have been waiting, praying for healing or for some other need in your life. I want to encourage you. Do not give up hope. Keep persevering and trusting God to help you in your time of need. Maybe you are like King David, at the end of your rope. In his despair, he was so desperate that he asked God to restore the sparkle in his eyes; otherwise, he felt he would ultimately die (Ps. 13:3). Nevertheless, he also knew deep within his heart that God would intervene. Two verses later, he wrote, "But I trust in your unfailing love; my heart rejoices in your salvation. I will sing the Lord's praise, for he has been good to me" (Ps. 13:5-6 NIV). Even when he felt as if his human flesh would not be able to make it one more mile, he assertively knew in his spirit that God would not fail.

One interesting aspect of this psalm is that David rejoiced in the midst of the trial. Rather than living in despair or simply throwing in the towel, he sang praises to the Lord. Instead of continuing to worry, he worshiped. His trust in the Lord outweighed his anxiety. Even before the Lord had rescued him, he acknowledged the Lord's unfailing love. Yes, his human flesh edged toward distress and concern, but ultimately, he wholeheartedly knew God would deliver him from his troubles. David was like someone who had fallen overboard from a ship, rejoicing over their rescue, even before someone had thrown them a life preserver. We should all follow the psalmist David's example. When we feel as if we are nearing the last thread of hope, we need to remember who created the threads of our lives in the first place. God created us, He loves us, and He will never forsake us. When we put our trust in Him, God will intervene on our behalf.

Due to our imperfections as human beings, it can be difficult for us to understand God's timing. We pray for particular needs, and we often expect an answer to come instantly. Nevertheless, God knows exactly what we need when we need it. Although we may not understand the reasons God would allow us to endure a trial, He has a purpose for each moment of our lives. As I was facing such a great trial, one passage of scripture encouraged me greatly. James 1:2-3 (NIV) says, "Consider it pure joy, my brothers and sisters, whenever you face trials of many kinds, because you know that the testing of your faith produces perseverance." I knew I needed to thank Him and praise Him in the midst of this trial, for I knew rejoicing in the midst of this disconcerting situation would strengthen my faith. I also knew it would give me a greater testimony than I could ever imagine. For every time we go through a fiery trial, we emerge as gold refined!

If you are going through a difficult situation in your life, look to God for strength. The Bible says, "Let us then approach God's throne of grace with confidence, so that we may receive mercy and find grace to help us in our time of need" (Heb. 4:16 NIV). I can tell you with full confidence that God answers prayer. Just as God answered my prayer and healed my body, He will answer your humble cry for help. He loves you more than you could ever imagine. Put your trust in Jesus Christ. He will comfort you, heal you, and rescue you. As First Peter 5:6-7 (NIV) says, "Humble yourselves, therefore, under God's mighty hand, that he may lift you up in due time. Cast all your anxiety on him because he cares for you."

Surrendering to God

"Trust in the Lord with all your heart; do not depend on your own understanding. Seek his will in all you do, and he will show you which path to take" (Prov. 3:5-6).

Although the notion of casting our cares on the Lord seems like a simple proposition, the literal act of letting go of our worries can often seem like an insurmountable task. Releasing our doubts and fears requires a complete surrender to God. Until we remove ourselves from the picture, fully relying on God to help us through every difficult situation we face in life, we will never have true peace. First Peter 5:7 does not tell us to cast a couple of our cares to the Lord and hold on to the rest for safekeeping. Consider someone who is taking a transatlantic flight. Instead of checking their three enormous pieces of luggage, they decide to bring them into the main cabin of the plane, along with their standard size carry-on luggage. Rather than obeying the baggage guidelines, they have the audacity to think they can hold them above their heads for the duration of the flight, since the bags will not fit in the overhead compartment. Surely, an airline would not tolerate such behavior on a flight, possibly resulting in the passenger's expulsion from the plane. Yet, if allowed to carry out their outrageous plan, they would quickly recognize the fact their arms would tire within minutes. The burden would be too heavy for them to endure for takeoff, much less the duration of the entire flight.

Similarly, many people try to hold on to too much figurative baggage, rather than turning it over to the Lord. They hold on to disappointments in their career, shortcomings in their marriage, and discouraging aspects of their health. If you could see all of the invisible baggage people carry around on a daily basis, it would look even more unreasonable than the person on the plane who brought an excessive amount of carry-on luggage. Every single person you meet has a story. Every person on this planet is often going through something. Every person has baggage. The difference between these individuals is what they choose to do with that baggage. Some people miserably lug it around all day, hauling various sorts of weighty bags like a perpetual bellhop. Others decide the load is too oppressive, so they stay home in lieu of living their lives, depressed and ready to throw in the towel. Still others take apostle Peter's advice to heart. As opposed to carrying around their burdens, they give all of their anxiety to the Lord, withholding nothing, which enables them to live a life of true freedom through Christ Jesus.

First Peter 5:6-7 (AMP) says, "Therefore humble yourselves under the mighty hand of God [set aside self-righteous pride], so that He may exalt you [to a place of honor in His service] at the appropriate time, casting all your cares [all your anxieties, all your worries, and all your concerns, once and for all] on Him, for He cares about you [with deepest affection, and watches over you very carefully]." Notice the first advice written here is to be humble. We cannot allow our pride to prevent us from coming to God for support. There is nothing to be gained by having a know-it-all attitude, or having the belief that we possess more wisdom than God. He wants us to call on Him for help. He is the Father who will always listen to His children's cries. When we come to Him humbly, then He will comfort us. Jesus said, "'Come to me, all of you who are weary and carry heavy burdens, and I will give you rest'" (Matt. 11:28). At the same time, we must give Him all of our burdens permanently. We cannot give Him all of our burdens today, only to pick them up again tomorrow. We must surrender all of our concerns to the Lord, never revisiting them again, trusting that He will work everything together for our good (Rom. 8:28).

Until we give God all of our burdens, we cannot sincerely worship Him. We must surrender everything in our lives that is displeasing to God, from our sinful ways to our worldly cares. We must surrender all of our burdens and sin, never keeping any souvenirs. Surrender is one of the most meaningful forms of worship. Carol Cymbala, director of The Brooklyn Tabernacle Choir, wrote, "A surrendered life is the key to experiencing God and being used by him to accomplish his purposes."[1] Surrendering one's life is a prerequisite to fulfilling God's will for our lives. We cannot hold on to our burdens while simultaneously taking hold of what God has in store for us. Nor can we primarily live according to our plans, only giving God a miniscule opportunity to guide us. I recall seeing bumper stickers on automobiles saying, "God is my copilot." Although this may sound good in theory, this approach to life is tremendously flawed. I desire for God to be my pilot, for He knows the precise moments I will encounter turbulence, and He will always guide me to a safe landing every single time. If you are trying to make God your copilot, I advise you to change seats. If we allow God to chart our course, we will never have to send out a "Mayday" distress signal. When we devote our entire being to the Lord, we can comfortably rest in His master plan for our lives.

Asa understood the importance of depending on God. His success as the King of Judah was because he commanded his constituents to obey the Lord's commands. Additionally, God's Word says he "removed the pagan shrines, as well as the incense altars from every one of Judah's towns. So Asa's kingdom enjoyed a period of peace" (2 Chron. 14:5). This time of peace did not come to fruition because King Asa was a good leader. The Lord granted his kingdom a period of rest because he surrendered his power to the Lord (2 Chron. 14:6). Surely, one of his most important acts as king was the removal of false gods from his kingdom. King Asa knew if they were going to worship the Lord, they would have to worship Him alone.

God honored his faithfulness when an army of one million men, led by an Ethiopian named Zerah, attacked Asa's armies totaling 580,000 men. In the face of an imminent war, Second Chronicles 14:11 says, "Asa cried out to the LORD his God, 'O LORD, no one but you can help the powerless against the mighty! Help us, O LORD our God, for we trust in you alone. It is in your name that we have come against this vast horde. O LORD, you are our God; do not let mere men prevail against you!'" Notice King Asa did not call upon his top army officials to develop a warfare strategy. When Asa said they trusted in God alone, he was not just speaking words that would sound impressive, never intending to act upon this declaration. Rather, he sincerely surrendered everything to the Lord. He turned over all control to God, confident that He would shield them from their enemy. King Asa did not place his trust in armies of men; he placed his trust in Almighty God.

If you are trying to make God your copilot, I advise you to change seats.

The Lord answered Asa's humble prayer. The Bible says, "The LORD defeated the Ethiopians in the presence of Asa and the army of Judah, and the enemy fled. Asa and his army pursued them as far as Gerar, and so many Ethiopians fell that they were unable to rally" (2 Chron. 14:12-13). Because King Asa completely relied on God to fight this battle for him, he was victorious. Alternatively, suppose he had told the Lord that his men could overcome one million Ethiopians on their own, never

seeking God for assistance. Surely, they might have all lost their lives that day. Instead, Asa knew their only hope was in the Lord, which is why his first course of action was to call on God to protect them. He knew they were defenseless on their own, but he knew the God they served was full of infinite power.

Like King Asa, can we honestly say that we trust in God alone? Alternatively, do we only trust in God when life gets too difficult for us to handle, striving to make it on our own when life is good? On the other hand, do we trust in God a little, while looking for some other person to provide extra support, as if God needed assistance? Asa knew God was the only One on whom he could depend. He did not wait until his encounter with the Ethiopian army to trust in the Lord. He rid his kingdom of idols, ensuring everyone relied on the only living God and worshiped Him alone. His dependency on God was the reason the Lord defeated the enemy on behalf of King Asa's warriors. He surrendered his army, his kingdom, and his very own life to the Lord. God spared him and his armies because he completely surrendered to the Lord, admitting his need for God.

Complete surrender is not about being carefree for a moment, but dependent on God for all eternity.

Unlike King Asa, many people find it difficult to depend on anyone else, especially God. Whether driven by fear, guilt, or pride, they avoid coming to the Lord for help, no matter how dire their situation might be. They follow their own path, often taking destructive detours en route to their destination. Along the way, they find the problems in life often escalate into more challenges than any one person could possibly handle on their own. They are like someone swimming upstream in a raging whitewater river without a raft, paddle, or life vest: a deadly combination. Living life this way is futile, as it will always result in a negative end. Instead, people need to rely fully on God in every part of life, trusting Him completely.

Until we surrender our own will to God, we cannot sincerely approach Him. Jesus said we should all come to Him as little children. He said, "'Let the children come to me. Don't stop them! For the Kingdom of Heaven belongs to those who are like these children'" (Matt. 19:14). Unless we humbly come to the Lord as a child, we will never inherit the Kingdom of God. Jesus said we must surrender ourselves to Him, trusting Him as a child trusts their loving father. We cannot allow the irrational thoughts placed in our minds by the enemy to distract us from our need for our Savior. Rather, we need to keep our minds on the Lord, looking to Him for strength and for wisdom.

Surrendering to God is not an option; it is a requirement for salvation. The things we have not surrendered to God are likely the things that hold us captive. When we give ourselves completely to Him, we will find that we, too, like King Asa, will be able to conquer any battle we face. God will walk ahead of us, fighting our battles, but we first must come to Him with the knowledge that we cannot make it on our own. Complete surrender is not about being carefree for a moment, but dependent on God for all eternity.

Chapter Eight

A Life of Worship

"Instead, you must worship Christ as Lord of your life. And if someone asks about your hope as a believer, always be ready to explain it" (1 Pet. 3:15).

Worship is not a Sunday morning ritual; worship is a lifestyle. Tozer believed that worship should be a Christian's full-time occupation. He was correct. Living a life of worship requires exclusive devotion to the Lord. You cannot be fully dedicated to God while also being fully committed to your family, friends, career, or other interests. God wants us to honor Him in everything we do, every day of our lives. True worship requires more than mindlessly going through the motions at church. We must prioritize ample time to study the Scriptures, seek Him earnestly in prayer, and sing joyful praises to Him. Psalm 16:11 (AMP) says, "In Your presence is fullness of joy." When we sincerely worship Him, He will give us never-ending joy. When we enter into His presence, our load will become lighter and our days will become brighter. God will help us focus on Him, even in the midst of our busy schedules. Despite what is going on in the world around us, we must live a life of worship, giving all of the glory and honor to Jesus Christ through every aspect of our existence.

Some people consider worship to be an act strictly reserved for church, or possibly something they do during some rarely available alone time at home. Although these encounters with God are certainly worthwhile, we must remember that worship can take place anywhere at any time. We can worship God during our commute to and from work. We can worship God while we clean the house, mow the lawn, or take a shower. In addition, we can worship God through the way we treat our spouse, the way we raise our children, and the way we love our neighbors as ourselves. We can worship God by seeking Him in the discouraging moments of life as well as in the joyful moments. To worship God in spirit and in truth means we have completely committed our lives to pleasing Him in all we do, from our smallest everyday tasks to our greatest responsibilities.

Worship has nothing to do with other people, but everything to do with our Creator.

Regrettably, there are people who cannot seem to grasp the literal concept of worship. Even in many churches today, the focus is on the worldly components of a worship service. Rather than giving the Holy Spirit the freedom to move in their midst, many church leaders focus more on following their carefully prepared program, vigilantly dotting every *i* and crossing every *t*. Meanwhile, they do not recognize the fact that worship is more than just singing another song, preaching another sermon, reciting another scripture, or saying another prayer. Their approach to worship closely resembles the words of the Lord: "'And their worship of me is nothing but man-made rules learned by rote'" (Isa. 29:13). Regardless of how godly the deacons and deaconesses of the church may be, or how dedicated the congregants may be when it comes to contributing their tithes and offerings, worship has nothing to do with other people, but everything to do with our Creator. In our giving to the church, to charities, or to a neighbor in need, our motivation must be pure. Our focus must be God. When we worship, we should be more concerned with what God is saying to us than what a pastor, deacon, or other church member may be doing or saying. We should also be more determined to follow God's commandments as opposed to man's customs and traditions. Worship is having an ongoing, divine connection with the only living God. Until we place our absolute focus on God Almighty, we will never be able to please Him entirely.

When God looks down upon the earth He created, I am certain He is greatly disappointed. While many individuals keep their focus on other people as opposed to looking to God, others focus on God, yet they are not coming to Him in a worshipful manner. He created us to worship Him, yet rather than millions of holy hands raised in worship to Him, many people angrily shake their fists at God, blaming Him for the great turmoil in the world. Other individuals do not hold up their hands in praise, but instead, they hold their hands out. They are waiting for God to give them what they want as if He is sitting in Heaven filling orders for all of their superfluous desires. Although God has given us everything we need, vast numbers of people reject the only One who can save them, simply because He does not respond in the way they think He should. When will they realize that He is the God who created the universe? When will they determine that God is not our servant? On the contrary, we are His servants, created to bring glory to His name. The one true living God deserves all of our praise.

Surprisingly, there are distracted individuals who become so involved in the event known as a worship service and attending details that they simultaneously forget the One they are actually worshiping. We cannot be overly concerned with the placement of the microphone stands, the choice of floral arrangements on the platform, or the layout of the church bulletin. Nor can we fret over the song leader's selection of songs, the way the deacon prayed over the offering, or the length of the pastor's sermon.

From the terrible temperature of the sanctuary to the perpetual pothole in the parking lot, it seems churchgoers today are in constant distress over peripheral matters. Instead of proclaiming praises, they are constructing complaints. None of these trivial matters has any correlation with worship. God's Word says worship should be "free from anger and controversy" (1 Tim. 2:8). If we sincerely desire to fellowship with God, we must get our eyes off the things in this world and keep our eyes on Him.

While there are millions of people who are traveling down the road that leads to destruction, millions of people daily worship the Lord in spirit and in truth. Jesus said, "'They are the kind of worshipers the Father seeks'" (John 4:23 NIV). God is not looking for half-hearted people who only want to be in His presence seeking Him out of desperation, nor is He looking for people who act like unruly children petitioning for some new object of their affection. He is searching for people who are devoted to serving Him with all of their heart, all of their mind, and all of their soul. There is no need to wait to worship God, or to be sought by Him, for Jesus said, "'A time is coming and has now come when the true worshipers will worship the Father'" (John 4:23 NIV). The time for us to worship our Heavenly Father wholeheartedly is now.

The time for us to worship our Heavenly Father wholeheartedly is now.

In the year 2000, Terry MacAlmon wrote a song titled, "This Is the Time." The lyrics of this song ring even truer now than they did twenty years ago. Over the course of time that I have been conducting research and writing this book, this particular song has become an anthem for me. I know in my heart that this

is the time for me to write this book on the importance of
worshiping God. Additionally, this is the time for every one of us
to worship the Lord in spirit and in truth. These are the days
when God is revealing Himself to those who will take heed. God
will move by His power to work in the hearts and lives of men,
women, and children around the globe when we worship Him in
spirit and in truth.

> This is the time
> When true worshipers will worship.
> These are the days
> When my Father's ways will be known to men.
> This is the hour
> When the Spirit's power will move again,
> As we worship You in spirit and in truth.
> Lord, we worship You in spirit and in truth.
> Lord, we worship You in spirit and in truth.

> *Chorus:*
> Holy, holy,
> Holy is Your name.
> Worthy, worthy,
> Let all the earth proclaim.
> Mighty, mighty,
> There is no God like You.
> And we worship You
> In spirit and in truth.[1]

True worshipers understand the critical need for worshiping
God. Without the Spirit of God in our lives, we are like an
automobile without fuel—stranded, unable to move, making zero
progress toward our ultimate destination. Nevertheless, if we
receive the Spirit of God through our worship, then we will start
to realize the magnitude of His power and might. We will find

that His Spirit will move in our lives. We will have the courage to forge on; ready to face whatever the enemy throws our way. As we sincerely worship God, we can have assurance that He will listen to both our prayers and our praises.

God is not an elusive being in the heavens who never takes time to care about His children. He is the Great I Am, always caring about every aspect of our lives. By refraining from listening to His still, small voice, we will miss tremendous blessings. Worship is the doorway by which we can receive these blessings. When we open our mouths, proclaiming His holy name, singing praises to the Lord, we will find that God will change our hearts. Anyone who hesitates to worship the Lord publicly is doing a disservice to himself or herself. Personally, I more closely relate to the psalmist David who wrote, "I will give you thanks in the great assembly; among the throngs I will praise you" (Ps. 35:18 NIV). We should all desire to give thanks to the Lord as we worship with fellow believers in one accord. For when we usher in the presence of the Lord, worshiping Him in spirit and in truth, our lives will never be the same again.

God's Word tells us how we should worship. First Timothy 2:8 says, "In every place of worship, I want men to pray with holy hands lifted up to God, free from anger and controversy." As we congregate together in church, or even as we sit on the side of our bed in the morning, praising the Lord for a brand new day, we should lift our hands to Heaven, giving God all of our praise. Some people are a little leery of lifting their hands, acting as if it is too public of an act. They may even squirm in the pew if the pastor asks them to raise one hand during a hymn of praise. Jesus Christ publicly died for us on a cross, stretching out His arms with nails piercing the palm of each hand. How great of a sacrifice is it for us simply to lift our hands in praise to Him? Certainly, we could never repay what He has done for us. Raising our hands in worship is one miniscule way we can honor Him, considering the magnitude of everything He has done for us.

Yet, countless people refrain from lifting up their hands because they are afraid other people may talk about them. Whether it is a concern of offending a congregation who may not believe in that style of worship or feeling as if raising their hands is a sign of weakness, they keep their hands frozen at their sides like a member of the Queen's Guard standing at attention at Buckingham Palace. While these Guardsmen perform an important role in protecting the Queen, there is no need for parishioners to remain unemotional when they are in the presence of Almighty God. He already knows our innermost thoughts and our deepest, darkest secrets. We have nothing to hide. He wants us to give Him our burdens, so He can give us comfort (Matt. 11:28). If we shed some tears in the process, He will understand. He loves us and cares about everything that concerns us, which is why we can open our hearts to Him, surrendering ourselves to His will, lifting our hands in praise to Him.

Nevertheless, some people come to church fatigued from a long workweek, making excuses that they are too tired to worship. When we examine First Timothy 2:8, it does not say to raise "holy hands" if you feel like it or if you have enough energy. Pastor Cymbala said, "One of the biggest hindrances to worship is people think they have to feel like they want to worship. That is the biggest device and lie of the enemy."[2] This "I don't feel like it" attitude would not have bided very well for someone like Noah. What if he had said, "I don't feel like building an ark," or "I'm too tired; besides, people will think I am insane." Surely, this perspective would have cost him his life and the lives of his immediate family and descendants as well. What would have happened if Moses had chosen not to lead the Israelites through the Red Sea? This noncompliant approach would likely have resulted in the death of the Israelites at the hands of the Egyptian soldiers. Furthermore, what if Jesus had told His Father that He did not feel like coming to earth to seek and save the lost, but He wanted to stay in Heaven instead. Ultimately, I could never picture Jesus talking to His Father this way. He was obedient, even unto death (Phil. 2:8). We need to have this same level of dedication when it comes to our relationship with our Heavenly Father. Sometimes, the one thing we may not feel like doing could be the one thing that will save our lives or even rescue others around us. All we have to do is take the first step by giving Him praise.

Sadly, some congregants are not too supportive of the concept of giving God praise. Some people grow uncomfortable when the praise and worship segment of a church service begins. They become nervous when asked to sing a congregational hymn. Part of their trepidation may be because their singing ability is not on par with others around them. Yet, Psalm 96:2 says, "Sing to the LORD; praise his name. Each day proclaim the good news that he saves." Notice this verse does not say, let all of the adequately auditioned soloists sing to the Lord. It plainly says, "Sing to the LORD." Every man, woman, boy, and girl on this planet should have a desire to sing glory to His name. He is the only One who deserves our praise. Concerning vocal talent, God's Word only tells us to "make a joyful noise unto the LORD" (Ps. 100:1 KJV). God does not hold the most talented singers or musicians in higher regard; He loves to hear all of us worship Him through psalms, hymns, and spiritual songs, singing and making melody in our hearts to the Lord (Eph. 5:19 KJV).

Although some people hesitate to sing aloud in church, singing praises is one of the most widespread methods of worship. Churches typically carve out time for at least three songs during a traditional Sunday service. There is one form of worship, though, often overlooked in the twenty-first century church: prayer. Unfortunately, the vast majority of people do not actually pray. Instead, they *say* prayers. Before you jump to conclusions, allow me to say that a well-written prayer can certainly touch the throne of Heaven, as evidenced by the oft-repeated Lord's

Prayer, which Jesus taught to His disciples. Although there is nothing wrong with reciting or reading a prayer, we also need to ensure that we actually spend time talking to God.

When I think about the close relationship that I have with my dad, my grandma, and other dear family and friends, I could not imagine only talking to them via a recitation or a script. We would never grow closer because everything I said to them would have to be pre-meditated, never spontaneously coming straight from my heart. In the same way, we need to ensure we are spending quality time in prayer, not just going to God with a laundry list of our problems and desires, but also taking time to praise His holy name from the depths of our souls.

When Jesus taught the disciples how to pray, He said they should begin their prayer by saying, "Our Father which art in heaven, Hallowed be thy name" (Matt. 6:9 KJV). Essentially, this verse is saying, *God, You are my Father in Heaven. I bless Your name.* We should have a desire to bless the name of the Lord continually, for He is worthy of all of the honor and glory. Jesus told His disciples they should end their prayer with these words: "For thine is the kingdom, and the power, and the glory, for ever. Amen" (Matt. 6:13 KJV). In the Lord's Prayer, Jesus confirmed that we should glorify our Heavenly Father, even when we pray. We should praise His holy name and give Him all of the glory as we pray and seek the Lord. Nonetheless, some churches feel that prayer is not as important as programs and preaching. This philosophy is unbiblical, for Jesus said, "My house is the house of prayer" (Luke 19:46 KJV). A pastor leading a church without substantial prayer time is like a pilot flying a helicopter without adequate fuel. Prayer is a necessary part of life, one that should always hold a place of absolute priority, both in the life of the church and in our own individual lives as well.

Even God's only Son prayed to His Father in Heaven on more than one occasion during His time on earth. He was known to get up before the break of dawn to pray (Mark 1:35). Before

He selected His twelve apostles, He prayed all night long (Luke 6:12). He prayed in the Garden of Gethsemane before His Crucifixion (Matt. 26:36). Luke 3:21-22 (AMP) says, "Now when all the people were baptized, Jesus was also baptized, and while He was praying, the [visible] heaven was opened, and the Holy Spirit descended on Him in bodily form like a dove, and a voice came from heaven, 'You are My Son, My Beloved, in You I am well-pleased *and* delighted!'" Even as John baptized Him, Jesus prayed. Afterward, God Himself spoke from Heaven, revealing His delight in His Son. These were not isolated incidents, for Luke 5:16 (NIV) says, "But Jesus often withdrew to lonely places and prayed." Jesus frequently spent time in prayer because He knew private communion with God was of utmost importance.

Just as God longed to hear from His Son, He also desires to hear from us. God wants worshipers who seek His face on a daily basis, sincerely desiring fellowship with Him. He wants us to worship Him, not just through raising our hands in worship, singing a song, or earnestly praying to Him, but also through how we live. Colossians 3:17 says, "And whatever you do or say, do it as a representative of the Lord Jesus, giving thanks through him to God the Father." From excelling in our workplaces to raising our children, everything we do should be a reflection of God's blessing upon our lives. People should be able to look at us, and without even having a lengthy conversation with us, know that we are representatives of Jesus Christ. They should see the light of Jesus Christ within us, shining like a bright beacon of hope in a world of darkness.

Furthermore, the Bible says we should honor God through our relationships with our spouses, children, and employers (Col. 3:18-22). God's Word says, "Obey your earthly masters in everything you do. Try to please them all the time, not just when they are watching you. Serve them sincerely because of your reverent fear of the Lord" (Col. 3:22). In order to worship the Lord through the way we live, we should respect our employers, always putting forth a one hundred percent effort. As a public school educator, I am so grateful that God has blessed me with such compassionate colleagues and administrators. I always strive to be an effective teacher, giving my all for my students and for my administration. Knowing my efforts are pleasing to the Lord makes my teaching career even more rewarding, for I know I am chiefly working for my Lord and Savior, Jesus Christ.

Pleasing the Lord

> *"Then the way you live will always honor and please the Lord, and your lives will produce every kind of good fruit. All the while, you will grow as you learn to know God better and better" (Col. 1:10).*

Living a life pleasing to the Lord is one of the greatest forms of worship. While there are many ways to worship the Lord, the way we live is one of the determining factors as to whether we will actually please the Lord. While worshiping God with our mouths on Sunday is important, what good is our worship if we are using our lips for gossiping, complaining, or cursing all through the week? God wants people who are fully devoted to Him, not people who only dedicate themselves to worship when the notion strikes them. First Thessalonians 4:7 says, "God has called us to live holy lives, not impure lives." God does not want us engaging in immoral behavior or carelessly gallivanting down a sinful path during the week, only to repeatedly ask for forgiveness every Sunday morning.

Some church denominations uphold a "once saved, always saved" doctrine, where a person can participate in sinful behavior and thoughts along their Christian walk, yet still have a ticket to Heaven comfortably resting in their back pocket. Ezekiel 3:20 (KJV) clearly warns of the danger "when a righteous man doth turn from his righteousness." Others use the illustration of the thief on the cross, whom Jesus told would be with Him that very day in paradise (Luke 23:43). While it is true that sinners can repent even on their deathbed, one cannot ignore the fact that God still desires for us to be holy just as He is holy (Lev. 11:45). Just because you could theoretically jump off a cliff into water more than one hundred feet below and not die on impact does not mean you should take the leap. The risk of fatality outweighs the possibility of survival. The mere fact that God, our Creator, is a forgiving God and will forgive even the vilest sinners does not mean someone should seek to break every law in His commandments, and then finally decide at the last minute to turn over a new leaf by turning to Christ. During the time of their reign of wickedness, their life could come to an abrupt end, never allowing the opportunity for a confession of their sins and acceptance of Christ to take place.

Every individual must personally call on the name of the Lord in order to receive the gift of salvation. Romans 10:13 (KJV) says, "For whosoever shall call upon the name of the Lord shall be saved." If an individual really calls on the Lord, a change will take place within their heart. Second Corinthians 5:17 (NIV) says, "Therefore, if anyone is in Christ, the new creation has come: The old has gone, the new is here!" Once this transformation has taken place, they should no longer have the same desire to engage in sinful behavior. Instead, their focus should be on glorifying the Lord through the way they live. Once we confess our sins and put our trust in Jesus Christ as our Lord and Savior, then we should always desire to follow His direction in our lives. When we do not follow His leading, our disobedience could lead to destruction.

Look at the parable Jesus told about the wise builder and the foolish builder. One person constructed their home on a solid rock, but the other person built their home on shifting sand. When the storms came upon them, the house erected on a firm foundation did not collapse, yet the house fabricated on sand fell to its demise. Jesus said whoever hears His teaching and "'doesn't obey it is foolish, like a person who builds a house on sand'" (Matt. 7:26). We should strive to live our lives like the wise builder; following God's teaching and obeying His commands. More than that, we must continue to live a godly life. If someone builds a house on a solid rock, only to move out and pursue ungodly interests, then they still would not be wise in the eyes of the Lord. He desires for us to live a life pleasing in His sight, one where we make wise choices and formulate decisions that honor Him in all we do.

The apostle Paul wrote, "He has saved us and called us to a holy life—not because of anything we have done but because of his own purpose and grace" (2 Tim. 1:9 NIV). While it is true that God wants us to live a sanctified life, we do not deserve this precious gift. The reason we can enjoy such a life is due to God's purpose for our lives and His infinite grace. God is the One who makes our lives possible. He created us for His glory (Isa. 43:7). With the knowledge that He created us to glorify Him, what reason would we possibly have to turn away from the very One who created us in His image? We did nothing to deserve His unmerited favor, yet He continues to pour out His blessings. We did nothing to receive the gift of eternal salvation, yet He still seeks the lost. We did nothing to earn His wondrous love, yet He will always love us more than we could ever begin to fathom. His continued compassion for us is an unmerited gift of grace.

You may be wondering why a king would bestow such a priceless gift upon you and me. Although it may be hard for us to understand, we can rest assured that Jesus Christ gave His life because of love (1 John 3:16). Because of His sacrifice, we can receive the gift of salvation. Romans 3:23 says we have all sinned and fallen short of God's glory. As a result, we all need a Savior. God sent His only Son to be the Savior for the world. When we accept Him as our Lord and Savior, we become a new creation (2

Cor. 5:17). While we could never repay the atonement for our sins, we can praise the Lord daily. My dad wrote a song titled, "Grace, So Amazing," concerning our need to worship the Lord to thank Him for His matchless grace. He deserves our praise for all eternity.

> He has raised me up and given me new life.
> He who knew no sin became my sacrifice.
> I've been born anew and seated with the King.
> Let me lift my voice; in worship, let me sing.
>
> Let me tell the world of Your special grace.
> Let them hear Your voice; let them see Your face.
> We lift up holy hands, for You have made them clean;
> We fellowship with Christ, our praise an offering.
>
> *Chorus:*
> Grace, so amazing, and how can it be,
> That the King of all kings would bleed and die for me.
> Jesus, I'll praise You for eternity.
> Grace, so amazing, was given to me.[3]

Every Sunday, many congregants around the world place their tithes and offerings in a basket, yet how many of them give an offering of praise? While it is good to provide financial support for your local church and other ministries, one offering is of greater importance to God than all of the silver and gold in this world. God desires our praise. He longs to hear from His children. He wants us to lift up holy hands as we magnify His wondrous name. When we worship the Lord, we can honor Him by thanking Him for His wonderful grace. A sacrifice of praise is one of the few actions that could even begin to say "thank you" for what God has done for you and me.

Let us consider that everything God has done for us has

been placed on one side of a balance scale. On the other side sits everything good we have done. Regardless of how many good deeds, how many charitable donations, or how many encouraging words we have shared, our side of the scale would not even lower the slightest bit. The Bible says our righteousness is as filthy rags (Isa. 64:6). Nothing we have done could ever compare to what God has done for us. He sent His only Son to die on a cross for our sins (John 3:16). His love for us outweighs the love of the entire world. Surely, we can lay aside anything that seeks to draw our attention elsewhere, solely taking time to worshipfully proclaim, "Jesus, I'll praise You for eternity. Grace, so amazing, was given to me."[4]

A sacrifice of praise is one of the few actions that could even begin to say "thank you" for what God has done for you and me.

When we worship in spirit and in truth, we have the precious opportunity to offer a sacrifice of praise to our Heavenly Father. While our worship could never reimburse Him for all that He has done for us, it is one way we can truly honor Him. As we lift our hands, sing praises to His name, and offer our hearts to Him, we can fellowship with Him sincerely. Our number one priority in life should be earnestly seeking God. We cannot allow any of our daily responsibilities to be a hindrance to our worship. Not even our family members can come between God and us. Jesus said, "'Anyone who loves their father or mother more than me is not worthy of me; anyone who loves their son or daughter more than me is not worthy of me. Whoever does not take up their cross and follow me is not worthy of me'" (Matt. 10:37-38 NIV). As someone who

immensely loves my father and grandmother unconditionally, I must admit there have been times when I know I have failed at keeping this command. It is easy to allow our loved ones to take precedence, even for a fleeting moment, over God, despite our best intentions. Yet Jesus has made it perfectly clear that we are to love Him above everyone else.

A popular saying today is, "Love you more." Ultimately, Jesus Christ is the One who really loves us more, and He is the only One whom we should love most. People, who know me well, know just how close of a father-daughter relationship I have with my dad. He is such a blessing to my life, and I thank the Lord for him every day. I am a daddy's girl through and through. Still, I should never put my dad ahead of Christ. Although the Bible does say we are to honor our parents (Exod. 20:12), Jesus clearly stated that we should never love them more than we love Him (Matt. 10:37). As Christians, we must put Jesus Christ first in our lives. What He wants us to do and where He wants us to go is of utmost importance. When we give Him the honor He so deserves and follow His master plan for our lives, then we will find we have more time to spend with our families because we will be spending less time trying to figure out our purpose in life. When we are fully devoted to the Lord, our priorities will be in the right place. Not only that, but our demeanor will be more godly, since we will be filled with His sweet spirit. We must love God more than all other people, places, or things.

As a little girl, I used to watch a Christian television program titled, *Joy Junction*. Their motto was, "Put God First." As Christians, we should all follow this slogan. Living a life of worship fundamentally starts with one single decision, and that decision is to put God first in everything we do. Until we can truly keep our eyes on Jesus, "the author and finisher of our faith; who for the joy that was set before him endured the cross, despising the shame, and is set down at the right hand of the throne of God" (Heb. 12:2 KJV), then we will never find complete fulfillment in life. We will be like so many people seeking momentary fulfillment, sin for a season, and worldly pleasures that can only provide temporary joy and imperfect peace. Only a relationship with the Almighty God can satisfy the longing in a person's soul. Only a person fully committed to Jesus Christ will truly be able to put God first in all they do. Only a life lived with Jesus Christ at the center will be pleasing to the Lord.

Chapter Nine

God Deserves the Glory

"As your name deserves, O God, you will be praised to the ends of the earth" (Ps. 48:10).

*N*ot too long ago, a young person told me they enjoyed singing in their church choir. As someone who sings with the Florida Worship Choir and Orchestra, I thought I could relate; that is, until the individual proceeded to explain the reason behind their love for being involved in the music ministry at their church. They emphatically stated, "Because I can receive all of the glory!"

Regrettably, this is becoming the norm in society today. People want all of the glory, whether they are at their workplace, at home, or even at church. Even among devout Christians who may be willing to let go of a portion of the glory, many of them refrain from giving away all of the praise. Tozer wrote, "We like to have a little glory for ourselves. We are willing to let God have most of it, but we want a commission, just a little bit for ourselves."[1] As imperfect human beings, how could we truly believe we deserve any glory at all? Isaiah 64:6 says, "We are all infected and impure with sin. When we display our righteous deeds, they are nothing but filthy rags." We have done nothing to deserve any honor whatsoever. On the contrary, all of our righteousness equates to soiled, unclean laundry. The most benevolent, respected, kindest person on earth is still a sinner in the eyes of God. Through the grace of God, we can find redemption for our sins. Because of the Lord, we have hope for the future. He is the One we should glorify, for He alone is worthy of our praise.

First Chronicles 16:29 says, "Give to the LORD the glory he deserves! Bring your offering and come into his presence. Worship the LORD in all his holy splendor." According to this scripture, we should be giving glory to the Lord. This verse does not say to give glory to the Lord *and* ourselves. Nor does it say to give glory to a celebrity, a politician, a pastor, or even our friends and family. This verse emphatically states that the Lord is the One who deserves the glory. When we do not direct all of the accolades to Him, Leonard Ravenhill said, "We steal the glory that belongs to God."[2] God is the only One we should worship when we come into His presence. He is the One we should focus on, whether we are in the midst of a worship service at church or in the middle of a busy workday at the office. We must enter into His presence and give God the glory every day.

> *God is the only One we should worship when we come into His presence.*

Even so, countless people ignore the fact that we are to give God praise for every single aspect of our lives. They disregard the idea that He is the One who enables us to accomplish everything we do, from opening our eyes when we awaken in the morning to closing our eyes when we go to bed at night. Many individuals constantly desire credit for everything they do, from making coffee at work to printing the church bulletins. While coworkers and congregants certainly appreciate these kind gestures, God's Word says, "Whatever you do, work at it with all your heart, as working for the Lord, not for human masters" (Col. 3:23 NIV).

We should never complete a task for the compliments we

will receive. Although positive feedback can encourage us to put forth our best effort, our motive should never be personal gain. Nonetheless, many people prefer receiving as opposed to giving. If they mow the church lawn, they expect to receive at least a pat on the back. If they cook a meal for someone who is homebound, they naturally anticipate a simple, "Thank you." Even if they stop to pray for someone in the hospital, they may think they deserve special recognition during the weekly church service. Yet, the Bible says everything we do should be for the Lord, not for acknowledgement from others.

Unfortunately, extrinsic rewards generally motivate people more than intrinsic ones. My students have frequently asked me what they will get if they help take down chairs or perform some other routine task in my classroom. My response has always been to tell them they will have the intrinsic satisfaction of knowing they helped their teacher. Expecting some sort of tangible reward, such as a piece of candy or a pencil, they complete the task with dismay. Still, I am grateful for these teachable moments when I can impart moral values in addition to the content I teach. While my students may only be children, many adults have the same desires. They live in a continuous state of expectancy and entitlement, feeling they deserve more than they have received. Their self-centered attitude bolsters their unrealistic desires, which causes them to lose sight of God and only look to their own interests. Yet, when they need something, they briefly remember God, only to tell Him what they want. They are not living to serve God, but only looking for God to serve them in a time of need. Furthermore, they are impatient when it comes to receiving His gracious benefits.

The world we live in today thrives on instant gratification, from fast-food restaurants that can deliver a three-course meal in minutes to cell phones that can produce information and answers to questions in a matter of seconds. Due to advancements in technology, patience has ultimately become a character trait from a bygone era. People no longer want to wait for anything. Some people even have this mentality when it comes to worshiping God in church. Although these churches and their congregants gladly post things like, "This is the day the Lord has made" and "Come, let us worship together," on social media and church marquees, their actions do not always coincide with these statements. For people who are supposedly fully committed to worshiping in the Lord's House, they seem to have more interest in getting *out* of the church sanctuary than they do remaining *in* the Lord's presence. Bradley Knight, music arranger, composer, and worship leader, once said these types of churches are interested in "microwave worship" as opposed to "Crockpot worship." Rather than allowing God to move in the midst of their services, they run through the program as quickly as possible, ensuring they release their congregants at a reasonable time. Otherwise, they run the risk of infringing on the church members' television viewing hours or interfering with a much-anticipated ball game. Without question, their priorities are not in the right order. Sitcoms and sports should never rank higher than giving praise to our Creator.

Even Jesus wondered why some people said they enjoyed worshiping the Lord, yet their actions showed something much different. The Lord said, "This people honoureth me with their lips, but their heart is far from me. Howbeit in vain do they worship me, teaching for doctrines the commandments of men" (Mark 7:6-7 KJV). Instead of focusing on the Word of God and the vital importance of worshiping the King of kings, people are often more in tune with the latest trends in running a church as a business with executive officers. While a church does require someone to oversee the finances and other business-related tasks, the church is more of a corporation of believers than it is a corporation of business. Despite that, many churches spend more time strategizing ways to present a program appealing to the masses than they do sharing the love of God. Borrowing popular aspects of secular entertainment venues, some churches have more of a club atmosphere instead of aspiring to be a house of prayer.

Nevertheless, they are simply catering to their clientele, for the majority of people would rather be entertained. From the perspective of many churchgoers, going to church should resemble an enjoyable concert followed by a motivational speaker. They want to leave the service feeling good about themselves. Their desire is to begin the workweek reenergized as they exit the sanctuary on a false spiritual high. While they may feel they were "worshiping in the spirit," one must question what spirit they were worshiping. Were they worshiping the Spirit of the Lord, or were they giving adoration to themselves, the pastor, the worship team, or some other aspect of the church service? Sometimes, people become oblivious to the fact that a church is not a concert venue or a social club. A church more closely resembles an emergency room in a hospital. Congregants enter the sanctuary broken, scarred, and discouraged from the events of the week. People are not in need of an entertainer; they need a Savior.

People are not in need of an entertainer; they need a Savior.

Jesus said, "'Healthy people don't need a doctor—sick people do'" (Matt. 9:12). He was referring to the lost. We are all sinners (Rom. 3:23). No one is perfect, except for Jesus Christ alone. That is why a church must encourage Christians and non-Christians alike, through the message of the Gospel of Jesus Christ. An upbeat song with a joyful sounding lyric cannot save someone. An inspirational message focused on living your best life cannot save someone. A friendship with a devout Christian in the church cannot save someone. The only road to eternal redemption is found through a relationship with Jesus Christ. Jesus said, "'I am the way, the truth, and the life. No one can come to the Father except through me'" (John 14:6). He is the only source of everlasting hope. He is the only way a person can receive the gift of salvation. He is the only avenue by which we can obtain eternal life.

The main mission of a church and its congregants should be to uplift the name above every other name, Jesus Christ. As God's Word says in Psalm 134:2 (NIV), "Lift up your hands in the sanctuary and praise the LORD." Our greatest desire should be to worship the Lord in all we do, whether we are sitting in a pew or standing on the platform. God created us for His glory (Isa. 43:7). He wants us to have fellowship with Him. When we worship the Lord in spirit and in truth, He will draw us close to Him. As James 4:8 (NIV) says, "Come close to God, and God will come close to you." There is never a time when believers should be moving away from God. Instead, we should always be striving to move closer to God, earnestly seeking His presence.

We should constantly be giving all of the glory to Jesus Christ, for He alone is worthy of all of our praise.

Rather than pushing God away when times are tough, we need to have the attitude of King David. When he found himself in tremendous trouble, he said, "O LORD, do not stay far away! You are my strength; come quickly to my aid!" (Ps. 22:19). Even when David felt as if God had abandoned him (Ps. 22:1), he still had assurance that God would help him. When David felt weak, he knew God would remain strong. Just as God helped

David, He will also help you and me, but it is up to us whether we call on Him for assistance. God will not force Himself on anyone, but He will respond to our call for help.

Unlike your friends and family who may be too busy to answer the telephone, God will always answer. The Lord said, "'When they call on me, I will answer; I will be with them in trouble. I will rescue and honor them'" (Ps. 91:15). He has promised that He will answer us when pray. When we closely examine this verse, we must acknowledge that His answer is dependent upon us calling on Him. Psalm 91:15 says, "'When they call on me,'" not when the Lord determines we need His providence. Although it is true that God knows our needs before we ask, He still requires that we bring our needs to Him. Hebrews 4:16 (KJV) says, "Let us therefore come boldly unto the throne of grace, that we may obtain mercy, and find grace to help in time of need." Receiving help from the Almighty God is reliant on us confidently taking the initiative to call on God for mercy and grace in our time of need. Once we humbly call on Him, then He will walk with us through the most trying circumstances life throws our way. When we look to Him for guidance, He will be with us always. When we worship Him, His sweet Spirit will be with us continually.

From the time we awaken in the morning until the time we go to sleep at night, we should constantly be giving all of the glory to Jesus Christ, for He alone is worthy of all of our praise. Psalm 100:2 says, "Worship the LORD with gladness. Come before him, singing with joy." Notice this verse does not say to worship the Lord with a sour look on your face. Nor does it say to come before Him with all of your complaints. As Christians, we should have joy-filled hearts, not gloom-laden faces. Yet some followers of Christ walk around acting as if the weight of the world is on their shoulders. To them, it seems as if they have to bear the entire burden alone, imagining an invisible barrier between them and God, but they have a flawed point of view. No matter what difficulties arise, God will be our strength and shield (Ps. 28:7). Rather than having a negative attitude, we should have an attitude of worship. Just as King David worshiped the Lord in the midst of his trials, we should also worship His holy name, even in the middle of disheartening conditions. Everyone who loves the Lord should be giving all glory to God at all times. For when we worship God, we can enter His presence with gladness in our hearts as we joyfully sing praises to His name. God deserves all of our honor and praise!

The King of Glory

"Who is this King of glory? The LORD *strong and mighty, the* LORD *mighty in battle" (Ps. 24:8 NIV).*

Earlier today, as I was standing at the kitchen sink washing our lunch dishes, I could not help but gaze out the window at the beauty of God's creation. The trees took on a more vibrant green than usual, and the sky was a more brilliant blue than an artist's paintbrush could ever portray. As I stood there, mindlessly cleaning up the kitchen, I began softly singing a song of praise, declaring the greatness of the Lord. As Psalm 47:2 (NIV) says, "For the LORD Most High is awesome, the great King over all the earth." The Lord is not simply another authority figure to add to the long list of prominent emperors and kings of this world. His excellent name is the only one worthy of our praise. Whether we are washing dishes, taking a walk, or driving down the road, we should always take the opportunity to sing of the goodness of the Lord.

Psalm 145:3 (NIV) says, "Great is the LORD and most worthy of praise; his greatness no one can fathom." No human mind could ever comprehend the vast nature of our Lord. His kingdom has no boundaries, for He rules over the heavens and the earth. In God's Word, we read, "Yours, LORD, is the greatness and the power and the glory and the majesty and the splendor, for everything in heaven and earth is yours" (1 Chron. 29:11 NIV). He is greater than anyone or anything on this earth. Even in His greatness, He cares about you and me. The King of glory loves us beyond our comprehension.

Jesus Christ is the King of all kings and the Lord of all lords. Psalm 24:10 (AMP) says, "He is the King of glory [who rules over all creation with His heavenly armies]." Christ does not rule over one particular region. He is the King over all the earth. Jesus is not an individual who has a self-centered desire for reverence. He is not like other rulers, impatiently waiting for their loyal subjects to obey them. Jesus Christ does not seek to control people under His authority, in the manner of other kings down through the ages. On the contrary, Jesus unconditionally loves every person on earth, even those who do not follow His commands.

When we consider the ultimate sacrifice Jesus made for each one of us, our response should be one of absolute thanksgiving and adoration.

According to First John 3:16, Christ's sacrifice for us embodies the meaning of genuine love. As a song I wrote a few years ago says, "He died upon the cross to show us how He loves."[3] Furthermore, God's Word says He did not merely give His life for people who love Him in return; rather, He gave His life for us when we were still sinners (Rom. 5:6). Jesus did not give His life for a particular group of people, nor was He concerned with anyone's socioeconomic status, ethnic

background, or cultural upbringing. The Bible says that Jesus gave His life to save everyone who is lost (Luke 19:10). We are all lost until we begin a sincere relationship with our Savior.

When we consider the ultimate sacrifice Jesus made for each one of us, our response should be one of absolute thanksgiving and adoration. As Revelation 1:5 says, "All glory to him who loves us and has freed us from our sins by shedding his blood for us." Rather than heeding the words of this scripture, though, many people today do not give Christ *any* glory, much less *all* of the glory. Nevertheless, Jesus Christ deserves all of our praise. Psalm 96:8 says, "Give to the LORD the glory he deserves!" No other soul is worthy of our praise. All of our admiration belongs to Him alone.

We worship God because He is worthy. We do not worship for material blessings or even spiritual fulfillment. We worship Him because He is worthy.

God deserves all of the glory, yet many people fail to grasp this reality. Instead of giving Him glory, they act like the Pharisee whom Jesus spoke about in one of His parables. Instead of giving God the credit for his own seemingly clean record, this man boasted about how he was different from everyone else, implying that he was better than the general population. He said, "'God, I thank you that I am not like other people—robbers, evildoers, adulterers—or even like this tax collector. I fast twice a week and give a tenth of all I get'" (Luke 18:11-12 NIV). Notice he did not thank God for helping him or guiding his footsteps to get to this point in his supposed spiritual journey. As an alternative, he essentially prayed a prayer about his own merits. He did not worship the Lord; instead, he prayed to boast about his self-professed godliness. Wiersbe wrote, "The Pharisees used prayer as a means of getting public recognition and not as a spiritual exercise to glorify God."[4] Like the other Pharisees, he refrained from asking for God's forgiveness, and he acted as a very self-centered, self-promoting religious figure. Rather than take a prideful approach, the tax collector was too ashamed even to turn his eyes toward Heaven. Instead of pointing out any good qualities he may have possessed, he beat his chest. Then, he said, "'God, have mercy on me, a sinner'" (Luke 18:13 NIV). What a stark contrast between these two men, all because one chose to keep some of the credit and the other humbly glorified God.

Although it is not a popular concept, humility is a necessary part of giving God all of the glory. The common way of thinking promotes the idea that each individual attains success singlehandedly. When someone thinks they can do everything on their own, they become like the Pharisee, boasting of their accomplishments and accolades. Instead, we need to be like the tax collector who meekly responded in a way that brought honor to God. Jesus said, "'I tell you that this man, rather than the other, went home justified before God. For all those who exalt themselves will be humbled, and those who humble themselves will be exalted'" (Luke 18:14 NIV). Instead of lifting up ourselves, we must lift up God.

Furthermore, we do not worship God for personal gain. We worship Him because He is God. My dad said, "We worship God because He is worthy. We do not worship for material blessings or even spiritual fulfillment. We worship Him because He is worthy." While it is true, David said he had "never seen the righteous forsaken or their children begging for bread," we do not glorify God because He meets our needs (Ps. 37:25 NIV). Nor do we honor God because He satisfies the deep longing within our soul. The paramount reason we worship God is that He alone is praiseworthy. No one else deserves the glory.

In spite of His majesty, hundreds of thousands of people still refuse to worship the Lord. They adamantly stand against all authority, even the authority of the King of glory. Consider Herod Agrippa I, who made it his mission in life to arrest followers of Jesus with the intent of harming them, sometimes to the point of death (Acts 12:1-2). What Herod failed to realize was that Jesus has all authority in Heaven and on earth (Matt. 28:18). The Lord is greater than all the earthly power that has ever been or will ever be. Although Herod may have planned to eradicate Christians as quickly as possible, he did not take into consideration that believers were continually praying for the safety of Herod's captives (Acts 12:5). One of his prisoners, Peter, encountered an angel of the Lord who led him safely past the guards and out of the jail onto the street (Acts 12:7-11). No harm came to Peter because of the power of Almighty God.

Show Christ; lift Him up for the entire world to see.

Herod ordered his guards executed following Peter's escape, and then Herod went to Caesarea for a time of reflection. Instead of calling on God, the only One who could help him, he returned to his throne dressed in his royal robes. As he addressed the citizens of his kingdom, they repeatedly shouted, "'It is the voice of a god and not of a man!'" (Acts 12:22 AMP). While Herod may have held the title of king in Tyre and Sidon, he was not a god. Rather than correcting the people listening to his oration, he continued to deliver his speech. Acts 12:23 (AMP) says, "And at once an angel of the Lord struck him down because he did not give God the glory [and instead permitted himself to be worshiped], and he was eaten by worms and died [five days later]." Herod suffered five long days and died because he did not give the glory to God. Instead, he accepted the glory as his own.

When we fail to recognize the awesome glory of God, we risk falling victim to accepting other people's praise. The acceptance of someone's adoration may seem like a trivial matter. Someone may receive an audience's applause for a presentation or performance, or they may receive a pat on the back when another person says, "Job well done." Although these actions may be innocent accolades on the part of the deliverer, how a person receives them is one of the most important factors. If someone tells their pastor, "Your message was inspiring," they are simply communicating the fact they were encouraged by the pastor's sermon. Yet, we should be uncomfortable hearing congregants say, "I enjoyed the message or music." Church should not be a performance or a show to promote human talent. Show Christ; lift Him up for the entire world to see.

We should only worship God. God has exclusive rights to our praise.

How a pastor responds to a congregant's complimentary remarks determines whether they direct the honor to the Lord. If the pastor boastfully says, "Thank you, I did my best to tell people what I thought they wanted to hear. I knew my words would encourage them," then the pastor has failed to give God the glory. A better response would be, "Thank you, but all of the praise goes to the Lord, for He is the One who helped me search the Scriptures, prepare the message, and deliver the words, which He knew the congregation needed to hear. I could never have done this on my own. He deserves all of the glory." While this is not a popular approach in churches today, the account of Herod makes it clear that we cannot afford to accept other people's admiration.

Similarly, we cannot direct our praise to anyone but God. Even the apostle John received rebuke for praising an angel in Heaven when he witnessed many prophetic signs and wonders. He wrote, "I fell down to worship at the feet of the angel who showed them to me. But he said, 'No, don't worship me. I am a servant of God, just like you and your brothers the prophets, as well as all who obey what is written in this book. Worship only God!'" (Rev. 22:8-9). Contrary to many large religious organizations, even the angels in Heaven do not merit our adoration. We do not worship angels. We do not worship saints or ancestors. We do not worship Mary or any member of the clergy. We worship God. No one deserves our glory and honor except for God. He is the only One we are to worship. As the angel said, we should only worship God. God has exclusive rights to our praise.

Do all you do in worship, and worship in all that you do.

The Bible tells us that God is love, but first, He is God. My dad wrote, "God is love. However, He is something before love. First and foremost, He is God. He is the almighty, eternal, omniscient, omnipresent, omnipotent, sovereign God."[5] God reigns over the entire universe. God does not want us to worship Him alongside other gods, other people, or any other entities. Deuteronomy 6:14-15 (NIV) says, "Do not follow other gods, the gods of the peoples around you; for the LORD your God, who is among you, is a jealous God and his anger will burn against you, and he will destroy you from the face of the land." Our Creator, God, requires that we only worship Him. Otherwise, we may find that our lives go into a downward tailspin, or even worse, end abruptly as with Herod Agrippa I.

We must heed the words of Psalm 115:1, which says, "Not to us, O LORD, not to us, but to your name goes all the glory for your unfailing love and faithfulness." This should be our daily prayer, whether we are laboring at our worksites, gathering at our churches, or relaxing at our homes. Regardless of where we are and what we are doing, we should always strive to give God all of the glory. Do all you do in worship, and worship in all that you do. He deserves all of our honor and praise. May we always honor His holy name as we worship the King of glory forevermore!

Chapter Ten

Worship in Heaven

"'Give glory to him. For the time has come when he will sit as judge. Worship him who made the heavens, the earth, the sea, and all the springs of water'" (Rev. 14:7).

For centuries, people have continually speculated as to what Heaven will be like. From artistic illustrations to poetic ballads, there are nearly as many portrayals of Heaven as there are people on earth. While many people ponder the many unknowns of this glorious place, we already know many details about the place God has prepared for all who love Him. Jesus said, "'My Father's house has many rooms; if that were not so, would I have told you that I am going there to prepare a place for you? And if I go and prepare a place for you, I will come back and take you to be with me that you also may be where I am'" (John 14:2-3 NIV). Based on this passage of scripture, we know we will have a place to live in Heaven. Although it is quite incredible to consider the fact that the Lord has been preparing a place for us for more than two thousand years, I am not personally preoccupied with seeing my heavenly living quarters. Nor am I concerned about walking through the gates of pearl (Rev. 21:21), taking a stroll on streets of gold (Rev. 21:21), or enjoying the beauty of the crystal sea (Rev. 4:6). When I enter into the splendor of Heaven, there is one place I long to be. My greatest desire is to worship around the throne of God, my Heavenly Father.

Worship in Heaven is described extensively in God's Word. Although our surroundings will be drastically different and our lives will be free from sorrow and pain, our primary purpose in Heaven will be very much the same as it is on earth, for our main activity in Heaven will be worshiping the One who created us in His image. Revelation 4:8 (KJV) says the four living creatures around the throne of God continuously say, "Holy, holy, holy, LORD God Almighty, which was, and is, and is to come." Likewise, the twenty-four elders sitting on the throne bow down to Him in worship as they say, "Thou art worthy, O Lord, to receive glory and honour and power: for thou hast created all things, and for thy pleasure they are and were created" (Rev. 4:11 KJV). These two verses alone should be enough to convince us that worship is an integral part of Heaven. Unlike the Heaven some people may picture in their minds, we will not be living as little cherubs floating on clouds as we play delicate songs on our harps. We will be worshiping the only true living God as we bow in His awesome presence.

Imagine the moment when we see Jesus Christ for the first time. None of the riches on this earth could ever compare to seeing the One who sacrificed His life for the forgiveness of our sins. Likewise, there is no individual, no matter how special they may be to us, who could compare to seeing our Lord and Savior. I know He will have my undivided attention. In fact, I could even be at a loss for words, considering the enormity of seeing Jesus for the first time. To kneel before the One who gave me life, and to worship in His presence face-to-face, will be the most glorious moment of my life. Surely, worshiping Jesus Christ will be my focus, for no one else deserves my praise.

Although I cannot speak for every Christian, I can say with complete assurance that seeing our Heavenly Father will outweigh every other aspect of Heaven. My loved ones, the beauty God has created, and every other part of this wondrous new home will be marvelous. Still, I look forward to singing praises to my Lord and Savior most of all. Every battle I have fought and every tear I have shed will have been worth it all when

I see Jesus Christ face-to-face. The mere fact that I will have all eternity to praise His holy name makes my heart rejoice, for my greatest desire is to worship the Savior of our souls, Jesus Christ. Unfortunately, not all Christians share this same perspective. I have heard people make comments like, "I wonder what sort of boat or car I will be driving in Heaven." Others wonder if they will be able to perfect their golf swing, sing like an angel, play any musical instrument without training or practice, or write the next great novel while in Heaven. Although we do not have all of the details when it comes to the activities in our eternal home, the Bible tells us that worship will be at the core of everything we do.

By contrast, there are Christians today who do not find joy in worshiping the King. They see church as an entertainment venue, where they can sit as a spectator, simply enjoying a good show. Their mind does not fully comprehend the fact that they have a Father in Heaven who desires to have fellowship with them. Instead of entering into His divine presence, they sit through the service using their electronic device to scroll through the latest updates posted on social media. Their boredom stems from the fact they have not made a real connection with our Lord Jesus Christ. Going to church alone cannot acquaint you with our Savior. Nurturing a meaningful relationship with Jesus is the only way even to begin to understand His vast domain. Rather than communing with the Holy Spirit, developing a deeper love of Christ and Him crucified, they prefer plugging in to their favorite online app on which they can mindlessly pass the time. How will someone with this mindset enjoy being in Heaven?

Tozer wisely remarked, "I can safely say, on the authority of all that is revealed in the Word of God, that any man or woman on this earth who is bored and turned off by worship is not ready for heaven."[1] If someone is bored on earth when it comes to worship, this individual has not spiritually matured enough in order to have the ability to appreciate worship, regardless of where this worship is taking place. People who exude boredom in a worship service are like children who edgily sit at the dinner table waiting for the very moment they can resume their playtime. Rather than being irritated, children need to enjoy the time they have to bond with their family. Likewise, we should value time spent in the awe-inspiring presence of the Lord. Only when we come to the realization of the utmost importance of worship will we begin to be ready for worship in Heaven. Worship is a precious gift, one that we should participate in on a daily basis.

> *Only when we come to the realization of the utmost importance of worship will we begin to be ready for worship in Heaven.*

Worship involves two-way communication. We must not only call on the Lord, but we need to listen to His gentle leading. Too many times, people come to the Lord during a time of worship, rattling off a lengthy list of prayers and praises, only to end their prayer time without ever hearing what the Lord is telling them. They come to God in an effort to ease their troubled minds, yet they may not even have faith to believe God will answer their prayer. As Ravenhill once said, "Many pray, but few have faith."[2] Jesus said if we have faith as small as a mustard seed, then we can move mountains and nothing will be impossible for us (Matt. 17:20). God does not desire for us simply to recite memorized prayers. There may be an occasional time and place for that, but He also wants us to come to Him, presenting our requests with emboldened faith. He wants us to come to Him as a child would come to their loving father. We should always be seeking His face in worshipful splendor.

Likewise, we must never forget that we are not the only ones who are seeking. The one true living God we seek is also seeking us. God's Word says, "'Yet a time is coming and has now come when the true worshipers will worship the Father in the Spirit and in truth, for they are the kind of worshipers the Father seeks. God is spirit, and his worshipers must worship in the Spirit and in truth'" (John 4:21-24 NIV). God is looking for people to worship Him. He longs for people to glorify His excellent name. He desires people to worship Him sincerely from their heart, not because someone tells them to raise their hands, sing a song, or recite a prayer. Genuine worship begins inside a person's spirit. God does not want half-hearted worshipers; He seeks people who give their all to Him, through their worship, through the way they live their lives, and through their obedience to His commands. God is looking for people who actually "get it," who truly know who God is. He is the Great I Am. We do not worship God because He is a powerful bully who demands worship. We worship God because we recognize Him as wonderful and worthy.

We worship God because we recognize Him as wonderful and worthy.

Consider King David's son, Solomon, whom the Lord chose to build His temple. David said to Solomon, "'And Solomon, my son, learn to know the God of your ancestors intimately. Worship and serve him with your whole heart and a willing mind. For the LORD sees every heart and knows every plan and thought. If you seek him, you will find him. But if you forsake him, he will reject you forever. So take this seriously. The LORD has chosen you to build a Temple as his sanctuary. Be strong, and do the work'" (1 Chron. 28:9-10). One could propose that the most important piece of advice given to

Solomon by David was when he told him to worship and serve the Lord earnestly and willingly. Nonetheless, Solomon failed to follow his father's counsel and angered the Lord by worshiping other gods, as we read in First Kings 11:10-13 (NIV):

> Although he had forbidden Solomon to follow other gods, Solomon did not keep the LORD's command. So the LORD said to Solomon, "Since this is your attitude and you have not kept my covenant and my decrees, which I commanded you, I will most certainly tear the kingdom away from you and give it to one of your subordinates. Nevertheless, for the sake of David your father, I will not do it during your lifetime. I will tear it out of the hand of your son. Yet I will not tear the whole kingdom from him, but will give him one tribe for the sake of David my servant and for the sake of Jerusalem, which I have chosen."

When an individual disobeys God's command, the negative effects can linger for multiple generations. In King Solomon's case, his son, the heir to the throne, lost control of most of the kingdom because of Solomon's idolatry. The only reason the Lord chose to give his son reign over one single tribe was due to his father David's devotion. Notice the Lord called David his servant. David served the Lord, just as he had instructed Solomon to do. When we serve the Lord, He will honor us for our service, just as He honored David by giving his grandson one tribe over which to rule. On the other hand, when we dishonor the Lord, He will discipline us for our unfaithfulness. Solomon chose to worship other gods instead of solely worshiping the one true God. His idolatrous behavior had negative effects on not only his son but future generations as well, all because he attempted to serve more than one master.

No one can serve God sincerely while serving something or

someone else simultaneously. Jesus said, "'No one can serve two masters. For you will hate one and love the other; you will be devoted to one and despise the other'" (Matt. 6:24). David understood the concept of only serving the living God. What would have happened if David had placed his family, his friends, his career, or even his own personal hobbies on equal footing with God? He would have grown to cherish one of them and loathe the others. Imagine if he had told the Lord, "I'm sorry, but I'm too busy to write the book of Psalms or to conquer Jerusalem." While this blasé attitude seems preposterous considering we are talking about a direction from God, there are people in the world today who daily abstain from following the will of God. We cannot serve God on Sunday and forget about His commandments throughout the week. Serving God with all of our heart is an eternal commitment, one that requires us to be "on-call" twenty-four hours a day, seven days a week.

No one can serve God sincerely while serving something or someone else simultaneously.

Our calling as Christians extends beyond the church sanctuary. As I am exiting a church building, I always love to see these words written on the inside of the doors: "You are now entering the mission field." How true this is! When someone stops us in the shopping center parking lot or on the metro station platform, we should be quick to deliver a word of encouragement, as opposed to a colorful dialogue of our weekly activities or a lengthy list of complaints. Although it is enjoyable to catch up with an old friend, comparing notes as to how things are going at our workplaces, or sharing the latest updates on our precious families, the most important thing we can do is share the love of Jesus Christ with them. By sharing a scripture, a hug, or even a smile, we could be the avenue by which God showers them with His perfect peace. Our mission in life should not be to lift up ourselves, but to lift up the name above all names, Jesus Christ. He has commissioned us to "'go into all the world and preach the Good News to everyone'" (Mark 16:15). The Great Commission is not the great suggestion. This verse does not say to share the Good News when you can find a convenient time. We are to tell others about the redeeming grace of our Lord Jesus Christ everywhere we go, every minute of every day. Each time we miss an opportunity to share the Gospel could result in someone leaving this earth without the saving knowledge of Jesus Christ.

> *Our mission in life should not be to lift up ourselves, but to lift up the name above all names, Jesus Christ.*

Rescue the Perishing

> *"You can be sure that whoever brings the sinner back from wandering will save that person from death and bring about the forgiveness of many sins" (James 5:20).*

Fanny Crosby wrote a song titled, "Rescue the Perishing." Unlike individuals who primarily seek to entertain people in many churches today, Crosby understood the urgent need for people to share the Gospel message with everyone they encounter. She believed Christ when He said, "'I am the way, the truth, and the life. No one can come to the Father except through me'" (John 14:6). The Bible says we are all born as sinners. More than 150,000 people die every day, nearly two per second. How many of them are dying without the knowledge of salvation found only through Jesus Christ? We must be the ones to tell them. We must help rescue the dying. I pray the words of the first verse of Crosby's song will inspire you to tell others about Jesus:

> Rescue the perishing,
> Care for the dying,
> Snatch them in pity from sin and the grave;
> Weep o'er the erring one,
> Lift up the fallen,
> Tell them of Jesus the mighty to save.[3]

Are you willing to help rescue those who are dying? Every single minute, approximately 105 people leave this earth. How many of them enter into eternity without having known Jesus Christ as their Lord and Savior? This fact alone should be enough to keep us awake at night, burdened by the critical need for us to share the Gospel. Knowing people are going to an eternal hell should continually motivate us to pray for the souls of the lost. Jesus said, "'The harvest is great, but the workers are few'" (Matt. 9:37). Even Jesus knew, over two thousand years ago, that people would not want to work for the cause of Christ. Most congregants want to sit in a padded pew and be entertained for sixty minutes on Sunday morning as they look forward to enjoying a delicious Sunday dinner followed by time in their recliner watching television. Instead, what if each of us decided to forgo the lavish Sunday dinner, only to grab a quick bite of food and then spend the afternoon passing out Gospel tracts in a shopping mall or a local park? What sort of impact could we have if we took time to witness to local nursing home residents or pray for patients in a nearby hospital? How would it affect our communities if every Christian fervently shared the Gospel, realizing the fact that people's lives are at stake? Salvation is truly a life and death matter. As Crosby's song so eloquently says, we must "rescue the perishing."[4] If we do not lift them up and "tell them of Jesus the mighty to save,"[5] who will? If we fail to share these words of life with them, they may never know of God's amazing grace.

Perhaps you are uncertain about the notion of walking up to complete strangers to tell them about the Lord. My dad and I write our own Gospel articles and tracts, sharing our testimonies of what God has done in our lives. Although the testimony of God's grace is truly powerful, the tracts are nothing fancy on their own merit. We print and fold them ourselves at home, so we have them at the ready for every cashier, every restaurant server, and every other person God places in our pathway. I have even developed the habit of giving one to our flight attendants and the pilot and co-pilot as I exit an airplane. Although I have given out tracts ever since I was a little girl, beginning with illustrated children's tracts, we find people are much more interested when we are able to say, "I wrote this myself." Upon first glance, many people will begin to turn down my offer as I hand it to them. As soon as I utter these four simple words, their demeanor changes. I am not giving them an invitation to join a religion nor a flyer about some cultic organization. I am sharing my own words, my testimony. I am delivering a personal account of what God has done for me, no strings attached. People are so receptive. What's more, they often begin reading the tract before I walk away. I cannot tell you the number of times I have stepped away, only to take a quick glance at them, thankful to the Lord when I see they are still intently reading my story. I even recall one particular server in a restaurant who stopped and read the entire tract right in the middle of a busy dinner service!

We have met several people who have written their own tracts, including an elderly lady who has copied her own testimony by hand by the hundreds in the pages of a small spiral notebook. Whether or not you write your own Gospel tracts, you can still share the Gospel. Tell someone about the valleys God has brought you through, how He healed you, or how He saved you. God may put someone in your path that may be going through a similar situation in their life; possibly, they may be hanging on to the last thread of hope. God can use your words to encourage them, letting them know there is eternal hope found only through Jesus Christ. You may be the first person to introduce them to our Lord and Savior. Romans 10:14 asks, "But how can they call on him to save them unless they believe in him? And how can they believe in him if they have never heard about him? And how can they hear about him unless someone tells them?" If a person has no knowledge of the God who loves them unconditionally, they may never call on Him. If they do not call on the only one true living God, then they will perish for all eternity. The Bible clearly states, "If you openly declare that Jesus is Lord and believe in your heart that God raised him from the dead, you will be saved" (Rom. 10:9). Every man, woman, and child must personally acknowledge the Lord Jesus Christ. However, if no one ever tells them about Jesus, they may be forever lost.

Regrettably, many people do not like to talk about the possibility of people being lost for all eternity. There are even many pastors standing behind pulpits around the world who never preach the entire Gospel. Desiring to make people feel good, they omit detailed images of hell, only wanting people to focus on the splendor of Heaven or a positive attitude in life. Yet, Jesus Himself spoke more about hell than He did of Heaven. The reason for this was very simple. Someone once asked Him if only a few people would find salvation. He replied, "'Make every effort to enter through the narrow door, because many, I tell you, will try to enter and will not be able to'" (Luke 13:24 NIV). Sorrowfully, there will likely be people who have sat in a church pew every Sunday, yet they will not be welcomed into the Kingdom of God. Some people have the perception they are a good person, so they convince themselves that God would have no choice but to let them walk through Heaven's gates. Jesus said that God will respond to many people who knock on His door, saying He does not know who they are (Luke 13:25). Jesus said, "'There will be weeping there, and gnashing of teeth, when you see Abraham, Isaac and Jacob and all the prophets in the kingdom of God, but you yourselves thrown out'" (Luke 13:28 NIV). Heaven and hell are not imaginary locations. They are real destinations. Every human being on this earth will one day stand at the door of eternity to either hear the words, "Well done, thou good and faithful servant," or "Depart from me" (Matt. 25:21, 41 KJV). Heaven will be a place of worship and joy in the presence of Jesus. Hell will be a place of cursing and separation from God.

I vividly recall standing by the bedside of a precious friend who was tottering between here and eternity. We had been friends for more than a decade, so she and I had shared countless conversations about work, family, and of course, the Gospel. She was a wonderful person with an altruistic heart as big as the ocean, but an allegiance to a religion based on false teaching and the traditions of men. As I looked down at her weakened state, I wondered if I had taken every opportunity to encourage her in the Lord. Had I really done all I could do to tell her about Jesus Christ? Before I left her hospital room, I prayed with her and shared the Gospel with her one last time, along with some encouraging scriptures. She could barely speak, but I knew she could hear based on her faint responses to questions I would ask. As I walked out of her hospital room, with tears welling up in my eyes, I prayed she would call out to Jesus Christ before she took her last breath on this earth. As she has since left this earthly home, I pray I see my dear friend in Heaven one glorious day.

My greatest desire in life is to share the Good News with as many people as I possibly can. Just as the Lord is patient with everyone, I do not want "anyone to perish, but everyone to come to repentance" (2 Pet. 3:9 NIV). God's Word says we should "make the most of every opportunity" we have to communicate with other people, so our conversation can "be always full of grace, seasoned with salt," so we will "know how to answer everyone" (Col. 4:5-6 NIV). When we meet someone new, our focus should not be on the latest weather report or news headline. Nor should we be concerned with telling them our life history or current state of affairs. Instead, we should be sharing the love of Jesus Christ with them. Jesus said, "'Enter through the narrow gate. For wide is the gate and broad is the road that leads to destruction, and many enter through it. But small is the gate and narrow the road that leads to life, and only a few find it'" (Matt. 7:13-14 NIV). Sorrowfully, Jesus has already confirmed the fact that most people will not find eternal salvation through Christ. Most people will continue traveling down the road of destruction, never to find the road that leads to eternal life.

We should endeavor to introduce everyone we meet to our Lord and Savior. Every time we put another activity first is precious time lost. When we refrain from making Jesus the topic of conversation, we lose an opportunity to help show someone the way to receive eternal salvation. We miss the chance to point someone toward the narrow road, the road that leads to Heaven. Every moment we speak to another person could be the last time we see him or her on this earth. We must make every day count.

Life is not about entertainment or pleasure. Nor is it about our careers, our automobiles, our homes, our pets, or even our friends and families. These things make life enjoyable, but they should always remain secondary to our primary calling on this earth. When we focus our lives on anything other than worshiping God and sharing the Good News, we will not be following the will of God. In addition, we will miss opportunities to help rescue those who are lost. Instead, let us all strive to be witnesses for Christ. Prayerfully, the people we witness to will one day join us as we worship in Heaven for all eternity. Let us all be workers in the field, as we continually seek opportunities to rescue the perishing, care for the dying, and tell everyone of Jesus Christ, who is mighty to save! Let us use our time and resources to reach the lost, so they will be able to worship with us in Heaven forever. As Luke 16:9 (NIV) says, "I tell you, use worldly wealth to gain friends for yourselves, so that when it is gone, you will be welcomed into eternal dwellings."

Chapter Eleven

The Spirit of the Living God

"'God is spirit [the Source of life, yet invisible to mankind], and those who worship Him must worship in spirit and truth'" (John 4:24 AMP).

There is only one true living God. Down through the ages, people have worshiped a plethora of false gods, but there is only one true living God. Jeremiah 10:10 says, "But the Lord is the only true God. He is the living God and the everlasting King!" Unlike the counterfeit gods, the one living God holds all power and authority in His hands. He is the Creator and Master of the universe. Even with His splendor and majesty, He loves us unconditionally. That is why He sent His only Son to die on a cross for the forgiveness of our sins. Only a loving, living God would go to such tremendous lengths for His children.

Perhaps you have only heard of a god of hate, as opposed to a god of love. I have met people who once only knew of a god of hate. This bred hatred in their own hearts, causing them to lash out at other people whose beliefs were different from their own. Through the grace of God, they discovered the love of Jesus Christ, turning their lives around, looking to the God of love for eternal hope. First John 4:8 says, "God is love." The only living God is love personified. He loves us beyond our comprehension. His love is "unfailing" (Deut. 7:9). He is filled with compassion. If you wonder why the one true God would love and care for imperfect people down here on earth, it is because He is our Heavenly Father. He cares about His children. He made us in His image. He is our Creator.

Although He has made His presence known to everyone on earth, there are people today who simply do not even believe in God. Rather than placing their trust in a higher authority, they deny the obvious fact this world even had a master designer. Instead of accepting the reality that everything designed and constructed has to have a designer and a constructor, they believe the world came into existence via some manner of random chemical, biological, evolutionary, or even extraterrestrial occurrence. Such notions are outright preposterous. My dad and I have an orange and white tabby cat named Morris. Domestic cats have thirty-two muscles in each ear. This is how our cat can move his ears independently from one another, listening to sounds in opposing directions. He can also fold his ears down, flat against his head, for protection. Such intricacy is not an accident. The master Creator, God, the same One who created you and me in His image, designed our furry friend.

Within our hearts is a jumbled nest of discontent that can only find fulfillment through sincere worship of God.

From the big bang theory to evolution, people still seem to think they have everything figured out. When asked questions concerning the numerous theories they may adopt, they seemingly have few answers regarding the finer details of their personally adopted philosophy. Inevitably, there comes a point where a person cannot explain an utter lie. Explosions create disorder, not order. Instead of evolution, we frequently see deterioration in our world today. Rather than producing evolutionary improvement, it seems that genetic mutations more often result in difficulty or worse. Buildings crumble. People grow old. While goodwill and morality are decreasing at drastic rates, animosity and immorality are increasing rapidly. The world as we know it is falling apart. Even so, people accept these false fabrications as facts so they can pursue their own desires, completely disregarding the One who created them. Nonetheless, the absolute fact remains that "God created the heavens and the earth" (Gen. 1:1). He is the One we should look to in a world of disorder. God is our only hope for the future.

Recently, I received a social media message from an individual who thought Christianity was a myth. I shared First Corinthians 2:14 (NIV) with them: "The person without the Spirit does not accept the things that come from the Spirit of God but considers them foolishness, and cannot understand them because they are discerned only through the Spirit." Their response was, "Fictional book." How sad it was to see how blind their heart was to the truth of the Gospel, even though God's Word says we can look at His creation and know He exists (Rom. 1:20). Instead of worshiping our Creator, some people put up a wall between themselves and God. They act as if they know more than God. Some deceived people even succumb to praying to birds, plants, or mountains before ever calling on God Almighty, just as His Word predicted. God did not create the heavens and the earth as objects of worship, but to serve as a means by which we might discover His awesome presence, bringing us to a place where we seek to worship Him. According to Tozer, "The purpose of nature is to lead us to the Creator and to worship Him. The purpose of man's feelings and emotions is to lead us to the One who implanted those within the heart of man, to the Creator."[1] God's creation is perfect, in that every piece of the puzzle plays a part in directing all human beings to worship their Creator. Within our hearts is a jumbled nest of discontent that can only find fulfillment through sincere worship of God.

Rather than worship the Almighty God, many people struggle through life, living according to false teachings, deceitful schemes, and even mythical and cultic belief systems. Some of them choose to follow their own path, hoping to one day become a god, be an angel, or simply die with no future hope of any kind. In addition, there are people who expect to return to earth as something other than a human being. The mere fact that someone would throw his or her life away, in lieu of accepting the truth of the one living God, reveals the extent to which man is lost. Truth itself is undesirable in some circles, for countless people do not even want to hear moral, sound advice. From sexual immorality to adulterous behavior and blasphemous language to murdering unborn infants through abortion, this entire world is on a steep moral decline.

When the direction of the world's moral compass has people applauding the abortion of millions of innocent children worldwide, one must question how we could ever recover from such an inhumane position. There is even political debate over providing medical care for the children who survive an attempted abortion. In modern times, people continue to worship Molech, the god of the Ammonites. Some of them do this knowingly and others likely know nothing of this god described in the Bible as "detestable" (1 Kings 11:5). Nevertheless, people daily sacrifice their children in the same manner as the Ammonites. Leviticus 18:21 (KJV) says, "And thou shalt not let any of thy seed pass through the fire to Molech, neither shalt thou profane the name of thy God: I am the LORD." Although God commanded the Ammonites not to sacrifice their children, the people ignored His direction, murdering their sons and daughters to appease this false god and to reduce the number of unwanted births resulting from promiscuous behavior. Likewise, tens of millions of people have aborted their babies over the last few decades. In modern times, people are not throwing their babies into the blazing stomach of a man-made god. Instead, they sacrifice their babies through the practice of abortion. They claim it is a "woman's right to choose," under the false pretense that a child is part of the woman's body, so she can do with it as she pleases. Basic science tells us that a child is a different person than its parents. Their genetic code is different.

Many things in society today grieve the Holy Spirit and hinder true worship. Since Roe v. Wade legalized abortion in 1973, to date close to sixty-two million innocent children's lives have been lost to abortion in the United States alone. Those who say it is a woman's right to choose should be thankful their own mother did not "choose" to end their life. The National Right to Life pro-life organization reports that ninety-three percent of all abortions in the United States occurred because of a woman's "social reasons," not the mother's health or rape and incest.[2] Maintaining a career, being a socialite, or simply avoiding motherhood are not valid reasons for murdering an unborn child. Someone recently told me abortion was acceptable because an unborn child is nothing more than a zygote. I must adamantly disagree. A human fetus is a human being with unique DNA, unlike that of his or her mother. Therefore, a fetus inside a mother's womb is not a piece of her body, but a unique person. Every child is created in God's image (Gen. 1:27) to worship God. Their life should not be intentionally destroyed. It is an affront to God's purpose and will.

Furthermore, there are even people who sit in Christian churches around the world who have little regard for what it means to live a Christian life. They sing "Victory in Jesus" on Sunday, only to feel defeated all week long. Likewise, they may place an envelope in the offering plate, supporting the local pregnancy care center or children's home, yet they promote or at least condone the alleged benefits of abortion throughout the week. Leviticus 20:4-5 says God will turn against anyone who aborts their child as well as anyone who turns their eyes away from the sin being committed within their community. As Christians, we cannot stand idly by, never taking a stand against the murder of innocent children. We must do all we can to advocate for the lives of these precious unborn babies. We cannot worship God in His beauty and holiness, while being conformed to the world and giving affirmation to wicked acts.

Unfortunately, many Christians take the stance of not wanting to get involved in other people's affairs. Still others have so many problems of their own that they have no time to spare in striving to encourage people with the love of the Lord. Worst of all, some Christians are Christians in name only. They go to church, looking like a Christian, only to go home and display depraved behaviors that would make most non-Christians shudder. Singing "Bless the Lord, O My Soul," on Sunday, does not erase dishonest dealings at one's workplace, nor does it cancel out the physical or emotional abuse a person may direct toward their spouse or children. Many Christians do not understand what being a Christian is about. Going to church is not what makes a person clean. Those who worship in spirit and in truth will continue to honor God in thought, word, and deed every day and in every situation. The word *Christian* is not some special anecdote that wipes away all of the mistakes a person makes during the week, so they can start out with a clean slate every Sunday morning. Being a Christian means a person is striving to be like Christ. Everything we do should be a reflection of His amazing, unconditional love. There should never be a time in our lives when someone could not look at us and say, "Something is different about them," and then walk away with the complete

> *Worship is not something we do occasionally; it is a new and living way of life, a heavenly perspective that permeates our being.*

realization that the difference is the Spirit of God living within our hearts. Worship is not something we do occasionally; it is a new and living way of life, a heavenly perspective that permeates our being. There is a strong connection between how we live and how we worship.

One thing many Christians often overlook is the fact that God is not only sitting on His throne in Heaven, but He also comes to us in the form of a Spirit. When we commit our lives to Christ and ask Him to come into our hearts to make us a new creation, the Spirit of God resides inside of us. You may be wondering how this affects your life. First John 4:4 says, "You have already won a victory over those people, because the Spirit who lives in you is greater than the spirit who lives in the world."

We do not have to worry about what people think about us, nor do we need to be concerned about the evil spirit, which may attack us. The Spirit of God is greater than everyone and everything else in the world. When we have the Spirit of the living God inside of us, we have nothing to fear. Because we have nothing to fear, we need to dedicate our lives to our

We must live in God's Spirit and in God's truth in order to worship God in spirit and in truth.

Heavenly Father. We cannot simply say we are devoting our lives to Him, and then merely live out our own desires, ignoring His will for our lives. We cannot accept the Spirit of God, yet act as if nothing in our spirit has changed. We must spend time worshiping Him, not just on Sunday, but all week long. We must live in God's Spirit and in God's truth in order to worship God in spirit and in truth.

What would be the point of only worshiping on Sunday, yet

forgoing worship the other six days of the week? To worship only on Sundays seems like a farce, where the worshiper may only appear to want other men and women to see them, to put on airs of being a "holy" person. Having traveled to over fifty-five countries and territories with my dad, I can tell you firsthand that many religions promote this sort of behavior. Some of them wear special garments to display their implied devotion to their god outwardly through elaborate pageantry. Others publicly recite prayers where everyone can see them, often using incense, prayer mats, or other tangible objects to make their religious devotion

> *Instead of listening to the world, we need to listen to the One who created the world.*

known. However, worship is not about putting on a display for other people, but giving exclusive praise to the Lord Jesus Christ. Jesus said, "'When you pray, don't be like the hypocrites who love to pray publicly on street corners and in the synagogues where everyone can see them'" (Matt. 6:5). Contrary to this highly visible approach to worship and prayer, God desires our worship to be personal, directed solely toward Him. In addition to worshiping in church, we should also be spending time in prayer, meditating on God's Word, and praising His holy name every second of our lives. He is the reason we are on this earth. Surely, we can take time each day to thank Him for everything He has done for us and to glorify Him for who He is. He deserves all of our adoration, not just when others are looking, but especially in the quiet moments of the day and night when no one else is around. It is in these moments of silence when we can often experience uninterrupted communion with God. When we fellowship with Him, He will speak to our hearts.

God wants to speak to us every day, but we are often too busy to hear His still, small voice. When we quiet our hearts and focus our minds completely on Him, the Holy Spirit will speak to us. Rather than listening to Him, we may find ourselves listening to a wide array of other sounds, from the news broadcast on television to the latest videos that are all the rage on social media. Whether it be our cell phone ringtone or the timer on the clothes dryer, it is hard to fathom just how many noises throughout the day can serve to distract us from the one single sound, which should take precedence in our lives. Unfortunately, we often allow the activity of this world to overshadow the presence of God. Instead of listening to the world, we need to listen to the One who created the world. His Spirit is all around us, willingly guiding us day by day. The Spirit of the only living God wants to reside in our hearts as an integral part of our daily existence. May we all fully commit ourselves to being devoted to our Heavenly Father, tuning our hearts and minds to His voice and not our own. He is the One on whom we should build our trust. Let us not depend on the world, but let us center our lives on the Spirit of God.

Worshiping in spirit and in truth requires complete surrender and dependence on God.

Nevertheless, this life of true worship is not appealing to all men. A rich young ruler was challenged to sell all his possessions and follow Christ (Mark 10:21). Because he held his riches in such high regard, the young man could not part with his wealth. Jesus said to His disciples that it was easier for a camel to go through the eye of a needle than for a rich person to enter the kingdom of God (Mark 10:25). Furthermore, He said it would actually be impossible without God's help (Mark 10:27). Those

who are independent, because of riches, intellectual attainment, political position, or social standing, simply find it very difficult to worship God. Worshiping in spirit and in truth requires complete surrender and dependence on God, yet many people prefer to retain their independence. Paul wrote in First Corinthians 1:27-29: "Instead, God chose things the world considers foolish in order to shame those who think they are wise. And he chose things that are powerless to shame those who are powerful. God chose things despised by the world, things counted as nothing at all, and used them to bring to nothing what the world considers important. As a result, no one can ever boast in the presence of God." For those who are "too smart for religion," God said His message would be foolishness to those who are perishing and that He will destroy the wisdom of the wise.

God Is Spirit

"Don't you know that you yourselves are God's temple and that God's Spirit dwells in your midst?" (1 Cor. 3:16 NIV).

God is not a human being. Counterfeit religions frequently teach of a god who is really a man. While it is true that we are made in the image of God; unfortunately, man has often made God in the image of man. God is not simply a good person who did some good deeds. Moreover, Jesus Christ was the only good and perfect person ever to walk upon the face of this earth. I am not a good person. You are not a good person. We are not good people. God's Word declares that we are all sinners (Rom. 3:23). Therefore, none of us could ever be good enough on our own. Jesus Christ is the only One who lived a sinless life. People often get angry with God and ask, "Why do bad things happen to good people?" Romans 3:10 (KJV) says, "There is none righteous, no, not one." In the history of the world, bad things only happened to one good person. Jesus Christ never sinned, yet He was crucified to redeem us from our sins. He is the Son of the one true living God. He came down from Heaven, leaving behind His Father's throne, humbling Himself by taking on the form of a servant (Phil. 2:7). God sent His only Son to earth because He knew we needed a Savior. Only a perfect sacrifice would be able to cleanse our sinful souls, so that we could be God's temple and that God's Spirit could dwell in us.

Worship is not something that happens in a building; worship is something that happens in a person. Worship is not external, where you sit in a pew and watch the people on the platform sing a beautiful song. Nor is it a time to rehearse mentally the activities of the upcoming week. Worship is a time set apart from everything else in this world, an opportunity where we can connect with our Lord and Savior on a deeper level, where His Spirit dwells within and we commune with Him. It is a time when we should lay aside our worries and cares, fully fixing our eyes on Jesus Christ. When we sing praises to Him, talk to Him, and listen to His voice, then we can experience true worship. As we engage in worship, lifting up holy hands, we will be ushered into the presence of the Almighty God. We will have a taste of lasting liberty, only found through the Spirit of the living God.

Second Corinthians 3:17-18 says, "For the Lord is the Spirit, and wherever the Spirit of the Lord is, there is freedom. So all of us who have had that veil removed can see and reflect the glory of the Lord. And the Lord—who is the Spirit—makes us more and more like him as we are changed into his glorious image." When we enter into a time of worship, God will give us freedom unlike any we have experienced before. Moreover, He will make us more like Him each time we encounter His gentle Spirit. As we place our complete trust in Him, then we will find that He will fill our minds, hearts, and souls with a peace beyond our comprehension. The freedom found through Christ is greater than any independence in the history of humanity. As John 8:36 (NIV) says, "'So if the Son sets you free, you will be free indeed.'" For those who have confessed their sins and put their trust in Jesus Christ, this freedom will last for all eternity.

The key to obtaining this ultimate freedom is simple enough for a child to understand, yet countless individuals miss the opportunity for God to set them free. Some people desire freedom, but they look for it in all of the wrong places. Others see freedom as a way to escape, yet they grow comfortable in their current situation, no matter how constricting the environment may become. Still other individuals believe they have freedom, even freedom through Christ, but their lifestyle, religion, or other entities overshadow this freedom to the point where they live in a cloud, unable to break away from the things that ensnare them.

God's Word plainly tells us how we can experience true freedom through Christ. It is not a secret. Galatians 3:22 says, "But the Scriptures declare that we are all prisoners of sin, so we receive God's promise of freedom only by believing in Jesus Christ." You may be wondering where this freedom comes from. God, our Creator, is the One who purchased our freedom. Ephesians 1:7 says, "He is so rich in kindness and grace that he purchased our freedom with the blood of his Son and forgave our sins." God loved us so much that He gave the life of His only Son, for He knew it would take a perfect sacrifice to redeem the sins of all humankind. Christ's sacrifice was a part of God's redemptive plan. Through God's great love, we can receive eternal forgiveness. His mercy and grace are never-ending.

God is far greater than man is. He created everything in the universe from nothing. Genesis 1:2 says, "The earth was formless and empty, and darkness covered the deep waters. And the Spirit of God was hovering over the surface of the waters." Before anything existed, God existed. As my dad has said on more than one occasion, God can even place Himself outside of the universe. He is not contained by any boundary. He can view His creation from a completely different perspective, which we can little imagine. God is all-powerful and all-knowing, yet He loves us more than we could ever comprehend.

God is not a man. He is Spirit. When we commit our lives to Christ, the Spirit of God will come and dwell inside of us. Romans 8:11 says, "The Spirit of God, who raised Jesus from the dead, lives in you." When we confess our sins and accept Jesus Christ as Lord, then all of the old things in our hearts and minds will pass away. The apostle Paul wrote of the way our point of view changes when we come to know the Lord in a personal way. He wrote, "How differently we know him now! This means that anyone who belongs to Christ has become a new person. The old life is gone; a new life has begun!" (2 Cor. 5:16-17). When the Spirit of God comes to live inside of us, we will no longer focus on the sinful nature with which we are born; instead, we will keep our eyes on the new life we have through Christ Jesus.

One of the greatest mistakes Christians make in their daily lives is not acknowledging the Spirit of God in their lives. They may attribute godly direction to utter coincidence, all the while missing the message God is trying to send. Amid the hustle and bustle of this busy world, which includes countless emails, text messages, television programs, and other distractions, it becomes so easy for us to miss His still, small voice. We cannot afford to overlook His gentle leading. Doing so could literally cost us our lives. I can think of many times when I had plans to go somewhere or do something, yet a gentle tugging in my heart said, *no*. Sometimes, a last minute change of plans could prevent us from being involved in a fatal accident or some other calamity. More than once, I have witnessed a horrible accident along the roadway, realizing I could have been involved if it had not been for an unexpected delay. When God leads, we need to learn to follow. He always knows where we need to be and when we need to be there. We need to trust Him at all times.

There are also times when God speaks to us on a spiritual level, through songs, sermons, and other means. I can recall an inspirational conversation with a dear friend of ours. When this particular friend speaks, I listen intently because God has given him godly wisdom. He was talking about our evangelistic work in Europe, as well as my *Be Encouraged* webcast. He said we would never know the impact of our ministry until we walk the streets of Heaven. As he spoke, he mentioned how people would come up to us, telling us they were there because we shared the Gospel with them. God has used this knowledge to motivate me not to lose heart when I encounter an obstacle on the road of life, but to strive to reach even more people with the Good News.

The Lord delights in our worship, and we can worship Him everywhere we go.

On December 31, 2019, I experienced another moment when I felt as if God was speaking to my spirit as I listened to Pastor Cymbala deliver a sermon titled, "A Year of Praise."[2] One of his scripture references was John 4:21-24. I could think of no other passage of scripture in the Bible that could have spoken to my heart in a greater way than the very text I have been reading, researching, and writing about since March of last year. Pastor Cymbala said, "This worship, this exalting the Lord in spirit and in truth, which brings such joy to Him, is the reason you were created."[3] God created us to worship Him. My heart's desire is to bring joy to my Heavenly Father, whether I am writing a book, singing a song, or teaching a class. For the Lord delights in our worship, and we can worship Him everywhere we go.

The Spirit of God is everywhere. The Lord's Spirit is not only present within our church sanctuaries, but He is also present within our homes, our businesses, our schools, and every other place we go (Josh. 1:9). There are times when we will easily recognize His Spirit, as I did on New Year's Eve last year. Other times, the overwhelming responsibilities we have in life will cause us to miss His presence completely. That is why it is vitally important for us to worship Him daily. Every breath we take is a gift from Him. Surely, we can utter a word of thanksgiving or a song of praise, even as we go about our daily routines. He deserves so much more than a brief stopover from us on Sunday morning. The Spirit of the living God lives within us. Everything we do should honor Him.

Nevertheless, countless people dishonor the Lord every chance they get. From sexual immorality to murderous abortions, countless individuals devalue the human body on a continual basis. God made us in His image, yet some people act as if their body strictly belongs to them, so they can liberally proceed according to their deviant desires. On the contrary, God's Word tells us that our bodies belong to God. First Corinthians 6:19-20 (NIV) says, "Do you not know that your bodies are temples of the Holy Spirit, who is in you, whom you have received from God? You are not your own; you were bought at a price. Therefore honor God with your bodies." Your body is literally a church. God did not give us a remarkable body, soul, and spirit so we could disgrace His holy name by sordidly manipulating our appearance, engaging in disgraceful sexual activities, or halting the divine miracle of birth. He has given us a miraculous body, so we can live a life pleasing to Him. The Spirit

> *The Spirit of the living God lives within us. Everything we do should honor Him.*

of God wants to reside within us, providing we embrace Him rather than reject Him.

Our lives belong to God. As Paul wrote, "You are not your own; you were bought at a price" (1 Cor. 6:20 NIV). Our lives were not free. The debt had to be paid. God's only Son, Jesus Christ, paid all of our debts when He gave His life on the cross for the forgiveness of all of our iniquities. Perhaps you are wondering how you could ever repay such a profound gift. That is the beauty of salvation. No monetary reimbursement is necessary. Still, as humans, we tend to have the skewed perception that nothing in life is free. Even the Israelites, after God had brought them out of slavery in Egypt, wanted to know what they could do to pay for their sins. They went so far as to ask if they should offer "thousands of rams," "ten thousand rivers of olive oil," or even their "firstborn children" (Mic. 6:7). They had the flawed belief that they had to give a tangible gift, but the Lord has need of nothing.

We cannot give material items to the Lord to repay Him for all He has done for us. My dad wrote a song titled, "What Can I Give to the King?" Many people spend countless hours trying to figure out what they can give the Lord. They may even try to earn His respect, hoping their good deeds or philanthropic gifts will suffice. While He does not need anything at all, we can and should always give Him our adoration. As my dad's song says, our praise is what we can give to the King of all kings.

Living in splendor in Heaven above,
Always abiding, His Father's great love,
Designer, Creator, He made everything.
So, what can I give to the King?

My earthly possessions would do Him no good.
His spirit won't dwell in houses of wood.
The greatest of wonders, we can't understand,

How God loves to live in the heart of a man.

Chorus:
What can I give to the King of all kings?
How can I show Him, what He means to me?
Through endless ages, His praises I'll sing,
And that's what I'll give to the King.[4]

We should all give everlasting praise to the King of kings, for He needs nothing else. Acts 17:25 clearly states, "Human hands can't serve his needs—for he has no needs. He himself gives life and breath to everything, and he satisfies every need." There are no material things on earth, which we can give the Lord. He already owns it all, including the cattle on a thousand hills (Ps. 50:10). Yet, there are particular things we can do to honor Him. The Lord responded to the Israelites, "'No, O people, the LORD has told you what is good, and this is what he requires of you: to do what is right, to love mercy, and to walk humbly with your God'" (Mic. 6:8). The way to honor the Spirit of God living inside of you is to do the right thing, be compassionate and forgiving, and follow the Lord in fellowship and humility. In today's society, many people strive to do what is right. Some people still treat others mercifully; nonetheless, it becomes more and more difficult to find individuals who are willing to walk humbly with God. There are people who want to walk with God only for other people to see them living a so-called holy life. Instead of humbly walking with God, they want to take the lead as if they are parading down Main Street. They think they will look strong to others if they put up a confident façade, ignoring the fact that their strength comes from the Lord and is not of themselves.

Even so, God is looking for men and women who will serve Him humbly. Jesus said, "'Blessed are the meek, for they will inherit the earth'" (Matt. 5:5 NIV). When we serve the Lord, not assuming we will receive anything in return for our service to Him, then we will be an heir to the entire world. Serving the Lord is not like a slave serving their master; serving the Lord is like a child honoring their father. When we devote our lives to Him, we will find that everything we need is available to us. He will take care of us, constantly watching over us. Someone might suggest humility is a sign of weakness, following up their comment by adding how God would give handouts to those who meekly come to Him. God's Word does not define an unassuming nature as weak. Consider Jesus Christ, who humbled Himself as a servant, "and being found in appearance as a man, he humbled himself by becoming obedient to death—even death on a cross!" (Phil. 2:8 NIV). If Jesus Christ, the King of kings and Lord of lords, could humble Himself, then how could any human being on earth consider themselves too high and mighty to come to the Lord with a humble spirit? Furthermore, Jesus was not weak, but stronger than the combined strength all of the people living on this earth. He was strong enough that He bore all of the sins, sicknesses, and diseases in the world—all at once! How can our burdens ever compare to the suffering that Christ endured?

Thus, we must walk humbly with Him, realizing we are nothing on our own. He is the source of our strength. There is no one like Him. Without the Lord, we could not get out of bed in the morning. He is the One who gives us life. His Spirit dwells within us, enabling us to accomplish everything from the most mundane tasks, like washing the car and doing the laundry, to more complex responsibilities, like nurturing children or running a corporation. Without the Spirit of the living God, life as we know it would cease. Let us lay aside our pride, our insecurities, and everything that weighs us down. Instead, let our focus be on the One who made all things. God is the source of life (John 4:24 AMP). Let us devote our lives to sincerely worshiping the one true living God as we live in fellowship with His Spirit!

Chapter Twelve

God Seeks True Worshipers

"'Yet a time is coming and has now come when the true worshipers will worship the Father in the Spirit and in truth, for they are the kind of worshipers the Father seeks'" (John 4:23 NIV).

*W*hat is truth? According to God's Word, Pilate is recorded as having asked Jesus this seemingly straightforward question (John 18:38). In order to answer this question, we must examine the words Jesus spoke, which prompted this very significant inquiry. Jesus said, "'I was born and came into the world to testify to the truth. All who love the truth recognize that what I say is true'" (John 18:37). If we actually value truth, the validity of the Gospel will be obvious. Jesus was born on this earth to bring the truth of God's Word to everyone who will believe. He did not come to earth so He could flaunt His wealth, for He did not even have a home in which to live when He was here on earth. He did not come to earth to gain notoriety, for the Bible says He "made himself of no reputation" and humbled Himself as a servant (Phil. 2:7 KJV). Luke 19:10 (KJV) says, "For the Son of man is come to seek and to save that which was lost." He came to provide a road to redemption for a world that is lost. He came to bring eternal life to a dying world. Without His testimony of the truth, the world would forever be in darkness. Jesus came to be the Light of the world. He came to save us from our sins (Tit. 2:14).

While Pilate may not have been comfortable with the notion of Jesus' purpose for coming to earth, it is certain that he understood the implications of Jesus' statement. In his heart, Pilate may have considered the possibility that Jesus' testimony was completely true, yet he also realized belief in such claims would place him in a precarious position with regard to the general population and especially the religious leaders. Still, upon asking Jesus to define *truth*, he approached the crowd outside and said to them, "'He is not guilty of any crime'" (John 18:38). Nevertheless, he ordered the Crucifixion of Jesus, not because of his own verdict concerning Jesus' innocence, but as a misguided effort to placate his corrupt constituents who raucously shouted, "'Crucify Him!'" (Matt. 27:22).

In the same manner, many people in churches today do not accept Jesus' words as being completely true. Jesus said many things that are not harmonious with contemporary man-centered culture. Contradictions like these make it difficult for new believers to sort out the truth of the Gospel from the heretical and unbiblical stances taken by many so-called Bible-believing Christians today. Rather than focus on the truth of God's Word, some churches make membership drives, mission statements, and financial goals the center of their attention. Although there may be a time and a place for these matters, the most important thing churches can do is to steer believers and non-believers alike to Jesus Christ, the only One who can save them. If we are not pointing people to Christ, everything else is for naught.

Jesus said, "I am the way, the truth, and the life: no man cometh unto the Father, but by me" (John 14:6 KJV). Going to church cannot grant you access to the Father. Jesus Christ is the only way by which we can come to our Heavenly Father. John chapter ten clearly teaches that Jesus is the door and those who attempt to gain entrance by any other means are thieves and robbers. A church devoid of this basic truth should repent or close its doors, because false teaching can do eternal damage. Nevertheless, we are all accountable to God, regardless of our church affiliation or lack thereof. God has made His existence evident to everyone, regardless of whether they go to church, read the Bible, or have even had the privilege of hearing someone preach the Gospel. Romans 1:19-20 says, "They know the truth about God because he has made it obvious to them. For ever since the world was created, people have seen the earth and sky. Through everything God made, they can clearly see his invisible qualities—his eternal power and divine nature. So they have no excuse for not knowing God." Every man, woman, boy, and girl is able to look at God's creation, keenly aware of the fact that a master designer built the universe. They only need to open their eyes to the visible truth, for His presence is all around us.

Regretfully, many people today are clueless when it comes to God's presence. Some of them are like Jacob when he awoke from his slumber and thought, "'Surely the LORD is in this place, and I was not aware of it'" (Gen. 28:16 NIV). They often stand in God's presence, yet they are completely oblivious to His awesome majesty. These same people are unaware of their need for His presence, while striving to fill this internal void with all sorts of man-made pleasures, even within their local church. From the pew to the platform, millions of people around the world spend many hours every year inside a church sanctuary. Although this should be a positive statistic, the motives behind church attendance in the twenty-first century do not always correlate with a genuine love for worshiping the Lord. Some people desire the social aspect of church, while many simply enjoy an hour or two of entertainment each week. Still other individuals attend church services to be in the public eye, hoping it will cast a positive light on their prominent status or help with business connections. Some pastors stand behind the pulpit feeding their aspirations of becoming a world-renowned personality. They may spend more time building their reputation than they do building their flock. With so many people coming to church for personal gain, no one should be surprised at the high number of churches with empty pews. Whether they admit it or not, people need something more than pomp and circumstance.

Just as a hungry infant needs its mother's milk, every person has an intrinsic hunger for spiritual food. In order to alleviate this yearning within us, we need to spend quality time in the presence of the Lord. Every one of us needs to know genuinely within our hearts that God, our Creator, loves us beyond measure. We also must love one another, just as God loves us. Churches must share these important truths with people attending worship services. First John 4:8 (KJV) says, "He that loveth not knoweth not God; for God is love." According to this scripture, congregants who do not love other parishioners do not even know God. How can we be effective witnesses for the Gospel if we portray someone who does not even know God? What good will it do to sit in a pew on Sunday if we do not even practice fundamental, godly principles such as loving our neighbors as ourselves? Sadly, many people in churches today have lost sight of these core Christian values, and others even dismiss the most important reason we should attend church.

Jesus said God's house is a "house of prayer" (Matt. 21:13 KJV). A church is not an entertainment venue or social clubhouse. Yet, the majority of churches today seem to be little more than social institutions. As Ravenhill wrote, "Today we seem much more interested in having churches air-conditioned than prayer-conditioned."[1] Pastors who lose sight of the importance of prayer within the four walls of the sanctuary are like someone trying to run a restaurant without having even one morsel of food in the kitchen. Just as they would not be able to keep their doors open for hungry patrons, a church without prayer might as well close its doors. Absurdly, some pastors say they are simply uncertain as to when they should incorporate a set "prayer time" into their already busy program. Meanwhile, God's Word says we should "pray continually" (1 Thess. 5:17 NIV). No matter what is on the schedule for a worship service, there should always be time to call upon the name of the Lord.

Otherwise, how can we expect to receive a spiritual blessing from our Heavenly Father? If we cannot even stop to talk to the Savior of our souls, why would we even hint at the notion of seeing our church being able to reach the lost for Christ? Anyone who believes a church can truly make an impact for eternity without prayer is gravely mistaken. The anointing of God's Spirit breaks the yoke of sin (Isa. 10:27). The power of God's anointing comes as we worship and wait in His presence.

God's power is far greater than anything that plugs into an electrical outlet.

The first believers fully understood the concept of a "house of prayer" (Matt. 21:13 KJV). Rather than becoming engrossed with the latest trends in church strategic planning, they "devoted themselves to the apostles' teaching and to fellowship, to the breaking of bread and to prayer" (Acts 2:42 NIV). Remember, these early Christians did not have the New Testament to share with other believers. There were no expensive sound systems or plush padded pews. Many of the methods and materials we love now simply did not exist in that day. Peter was preaching without any fog machines or automated theatrical lighting, but he saw thousands of souls saved by the power of the Holy Spirit. God's power is far greater than anything that plugs into an electrical outlet.

Although the absence of these modern amenities could certainly put a damper on church attendance today, the early Christian church was not concerned with the creature comforts of their surroundings. Instead, they were faithful to the One who created them. They enjoyed fellowship together every day, meeting at the temple and in each other's homes (Acts 2:46). As

the people gathered, they studied the teachings of the apostles, which would later become part of the New Testament. They shared meals together, encouraging one another through their conversations. Still, their devotion to prayer was undoubtedly the key to the enormous impact they made on those around them. Similar to a remark delivered by an attendee at the Finney Revival in New England, these early Christians would likely have exclaimed, "God is in this place!" They knew the Lord's presence was necessary for worship, and they fully understood the need for prayer to be an integral part of their time together.

As Christians, we should not be serving ourselves, but serving God.

Even in the last few centuries, there have been devoted individuals who followed the examples of the early believers, fervently pursuing God through a loyal commitment to prayer. John Fletcher, one of the most prominent theologians of the Methodist movement, spent so much time in prayer each day that he stained the walls of his prayer room with his breath and left indentations on the floor where he knelt in prayer. Likewise, renowned author, attorney, and clergy, E.M. Bounds, began his prayer time at four o'clock in the morning, devotedly spending three hours in prayer every day. What would happen if Christians today would spend even one hour a day, praying for the Lord's protection and guidance? Although there are still prayer warriors around the world who faithfully go to the throne of grace, there are also people who say they love the Lord, yet the only time they talk to Him is when they say grace over their meals. There are even people in full-time ministry who focus on climbing the ladder of success more than they spend time in prayer.

For many ministries today, they measure their success by church membership or financial status. Some churches compete to see who can have the largest building, the most talented worship team, or the best sounding band. While these things may be pleasant, they all miss the mark. As Christians, we should not be serving ourselves, but serving God. Additionally, we should be ministering to the needs of the people in our communities. The early Christians understood this, which is why they often broke bread and prayed together. They realized their need for God's anointing upon their ministry. These individuals knew they could not accomplish anything on their own. God honored their faithfulness. Acts 2:47 (NIV) says, "And the Lord added to their number daily those who were being saved." As witnesses for Christ, they shared the gift of salvation. The people God placed in their paths were receptive to the Gospel, even without the fanfare we have in churches today. If the early Christians could see people saved on a daily basis, what is our excuse in modern times?

God has called each of us to go forth and proclaim the Gospel to all creation (Mark 16:15). God did not give us this directive as a suggestion, in case we find time in our busy schedules to witness to someone. We should make it our greatest mission in life to share the love of Jesus Christ with everyone we meet. Nothing else will change a life for all eternity. The early believers understood this, which is why the Bible says they were devoted to being witnesses for Christ. What do witnesses do? They tell what they have seen and heard. The first Christians were not paralyzed by the absence of the New Testament, for they simply told others what they had witnessed. Surely, these eyewitness accounts were more effective than if they had merely been sharing a meaningless pamphlet soliciting donations for some corporate religious institution. They likely told people about miracles they had seen or explained Jesus' teachings as related to them by the apostles. Could you imagine what it must have been like for people to hear about people raised from the dead and the blind made to see? Even today, hearing miraculous accounts of God's power causes our own faith to strengthen. So why should we refrain from telling our own stories? Why should we refuse to share the only eternally life-changing news with everyone we meet?

Perhaps you are considering the possibility of witnessing to someone God has already placed in your path. You might be hesitant, uncertain how they will react. You may feel unqualified, taking into account the fact you do not hold a degree in theology or ordination from a seminary. The early Christians did not go to Bible school, nor did they even hold a complete Bible in their hands. Yet they were able to witness to others, sharing the wondrous Good News, ultimately seeing people's lives changed as they came to accept salvation through Jesus Christ our Lord. These were ordinary people like you and me. Yet, Acts 17:6 (KJV) says they "turned the world upside down." They did not let anything hinder them, for they wanted to please God in every aspect of their lives. Like the members of the early church, I want to be one of God's servants. What does a servant do? They work hard for their master. We need to strive to give our all for Christ. He gave His life for us when we were still sinners (Rom. 5:8).

You and I did nothing to deserve this wonderful gift of grace. Ephesians 2:8-9 (NIV) says, "For it is by grace you have been saved, through faith—and this is not from yourselves, it is the gift of God—not by works, so that no one can boast." If we had to rely on the things we could give to the Lord, we would be in an eternally hopeless situation. We have nothing of value to offer to Jesus Christ that could ever repay Him for the sacrifice He made for us. It is only because of God's matchless grace that we can receive the gift of eternal salvation. God's Word says Jesus' blood was "'poured out as a sacrifice for many'" (Mark 14:24). He did not hold anything back. My dad wrote a song several years ago, which exemplifies the sacrifice our Lord and

Savior gave for us, for Jesus Christ truly gave His all on the cross.

> He knew me long before I took a breath.
> All my days of life are numbered
> 'Till I close my eyes in death.
> He knew I'd need a Savior;
> He knew that I would fall.
> When I had nothing to give,
> He gave His all.

> "All have sinned," the Bible does declare.
> What a miracle of grace
> That our holy God would care.
> "For God so loved the world"
> To redeem man from the fall.
> When I had nothing to give,
> He gave His all.

> *Chorus:*
> In mercy, love, and grace,
> The Father reaches down to man.
> His cleansing blood upon the cross
> To seal redemption's plan.
> As He looked down through the ages,
> He knew that I would fall.
> When I had nothing to give,
> He gave His all.[2]

Jesus Christ truly gave His all for you and me. The Bible says Jesus "made himself of no reputation, and took upon him the form of a servant, and was made in the likeness of men" (Phil. 2:7 KJV). If Jesus, the King of kings and Lord of lords, could take on the form of a servant, then why do we have such a difficult time serving Him? Some people may dispute this question, saying, "Wait a minute now, I serve the Lord." While an individual may faithfully attend church, place a percentage of their income in the offering, or even teach a Sunday school class, God has called us all to do more than serve our local church. Sometimes, the greatest ministry opportunities are not always so comfortable or even attractive, but they come with greater rewards than anything this world has to offer.

One summer, my dad and I met a homeless man living on the streets of New York City. Due to some poor choices he had made in his life, this former high school valedictorian was battling significant medical issues and begging for food in downtown Brooklyn. I cannot tell you how heart wrenching it was to hear this senior citizen repeatedly say, "I just want a fish sandwich." A fish sandwich, something my dad and I could buy anytime. For this man, it was not so easily attainable. As we walked into a fast-food restaurant, I was saddened once more when he told us the manager would not allow him to enter due to a previous incident. My dad and I stepped up to the counter, ordered a fish sandwich, an order of fries, and a soft drink. When we turned around, the man had followed us and come inside anyway. Refusing to sit down, he proceeded to attempt to eat his meal standing up, which was very difficult for him. Soon he made his way outside, where my dad suggested he sit down on a nearby bench. All of the sudden, he started yelling, "You can't tell me what to do!" My dad calmly told him that he simply did not want him to drop the fish sandwich we gave him. Then, the man asked, "You bought me this sandwich?" His mind was so confused; it was sad and very troubling to observe.

The entire encounter with this man was certainly out of the ordinary, but I know God ordered our steps as we crossed paths that day. Before we parted ways, we prayed with him and gave him some Gospel tracts. I will always remember one of the things he said to us. He said he was not worth anything. I told him he was special in God's eyes, and God loved him so very much.

Even with the communicative obstacles, considering his unstable mental condition, we did our best to share the Gospel of Jesus Christ with him. Although we may never see him again on this earth, I pray we see him in Heaven one glorious day.

When we go about the Lord's business, we may find ourselves speaking to a crowd from the platform of a prominent church, or we may also find ourselves on the streets of a metropolis or village, trying to witness to someone who does not even have a roof over their head. The one thing we need to remember, though, is that God loves a homeless man or woman just as much as a wealthy executive in a corporate office. Showing little compassion, some church members cringe when someone unkempt or poorly dressed enters into the church sanctuary. Yet, God does not view people the way we do. He does not focus on someone's financial resources, cultural background, or even celebrity status. Where we may treat someone differently based on one or more of these factors, God sees us all on an even playing field. We need to be like Him, loving all of our neighbors as ourselves. Jesus did not say to witness to a few nicely dressed people, or to stay in one little clique of friends and family. He said we should go into the entire world, and share the Gospel with all creation (Mark 16:15). This verse says *all* creation, not simply the beautiful parts of it.

Regrettably, many churches cater to the pleasure of their congregation rather than ministering to the needs of their community. From banquet halls and bus trips to retreat and recreation centers, they constantly spend their resources to fulfill the desires of their loyal membership instead of exploring the ways they can take the Gospel to the lost right within their own neighborhoods. Still others realize the positive impact they can have on their surrounding areas. On one of our journeys to Eastern Europe, it was a privilege for my dad and me to join Peter Rong, pastor of Spiritual Revival Baptist Church, in Bucharest, Romania, for a day of evangelism in the local neighborhood and a nearby park. Nothing could have prepared me for the warm reception we received from complete strangers. With the pastor serving as our interpreter, we walked up to men and women, young and old, sharing the Good News of the Gospel and asking if we could pray for them as God's Spirit directed. Without exception, they were grateful for our prayers, our compassion, and most of all, our time. I will always recall a group of precious children whom I gave Gospel tracts to in the park. They seemed astonished that I would give them something free of charge. I pray God has spoken to their hearts since that sunny afternoon in a picturesque park in Bucharest.

Every day, God places ministry opportunities in our path. You may not be a professional pastor, an evangelist, or a missionary. But you must be a willing vessel, always ready and eager to share the Gospel, even in the most unlikely places. My dad and I have met so many people who needed a word of encouragement. One day, we were having lunch at a popular restaurant. At the end of the meal, my dad paid the bill and handed our waiter a Gospel tract. As soon as he saw the title of the tract, he literally broke down in tears. As he regained his composure, he said his family had nearly disowned him, all because he was "just a waiter." Others in his family had careers they considered more prestigious. The fact he was unable to travel home for the Thanksgiving holiday served to make him even more downcast. He said he had really had a rough time lately, thinking about all of these things, and the encouragement we provided him meant so very much. How humbling it was to see how God ordered our steps, bringing us to the right restaurant, at the right time, at the table served by this particular waiter.

In the Netherlands, we had another unique experience while witnessing to a complete stranger who would soon become a cherished friend. During some free time, we toured the Royal Delft earthenware factory and museum. At the end of our visit, I gave a Gospel tract containing my testimony to one of the employees there. A couple of days later, I received a note from them, letting me know what an encouragement my message was to them, especially on that particular day. In the communication that followed, I learned they had been going through some very tough times personally. Since then, we have kept in touch, and I strive to encourage this individual at every opportunity.

God knows what every person is going through. As such, He also knows when we need to share an inspirational message, even with someone we do not know. If we ignore His leading, we will miss being a blessing to someone else and even receiving a blessing ourselves. Everyone has a story, yet many times, we go on about our day, unwilling to spend even one extra minute to have a conversation with someone about the Lord. Instead, we need to take time to minister to others. Colossians 3:17 (AMP) says, "Whatever you do [no matter what it is] in word or deed, do everything in the name of the Lord Jesus [and in dependence on Him], giving thanks to God the Father through Him." Whether we encourage someone in the checkout lane at the grocery store, give a Gospel tract to a server at a café, or even have a quick conversation with an individual on the metro platform, God can use us to make a difference in their day, and perhaps, even their lives. We should do everything in the name of the Lord, relying on Him to guide our steps. When we trust Him completely, I can tell you from personal experience that He will use us in ways we could not even begin to imagine. Let us boldly proclaim the goodness of God and exalt the name of Jesus Christ in our daily conversations.

Furthermore, this scripture says we should give thanks to God. Once more, we see the importance of being thankful. We cannot be like so many people in the world, allowing a sense of entitlement to reign supreme. Although society may tell you otherwise, we do not deserve anything whatsoever. It is only through the grace of God that we have anything at all. On our own merit, we deserve nothing good. God is the One who supplies our every need, from the bed we slept in last night to the breakfast we enjoyed this morning. Not only that, but He is the One who awakened us. Not too long ago, someone told me every day was terrible. I quickly reminded them every day is a good day, even though there could be some tough moments. The greatest gift of all is that God allowed us to live another day for His glory.

Rather than questioning everything God does, we need to realize that everything God does is perfect.

While I will never be able to understand God's ways completely, I often wonder what He thinks when He looks down from Heaven upon His creation. Here we have an infinite number of blessings, including oxygen, water, food, shelter, and so much more, not to mention our family, friends, colleagues, and acquaintances. Yet, people still desire more. They want greater salaries, nicer automobiles, larger homes, newer electronic gadgets, fancier clothing, and more elaborate food. Even people who receive a blessing immediately tend to desire something superior, holding the impression that life owes it to them. Children who receive a new toy generally lose interest within a short span of time, and then they see something else in the store and may even have a temper tantrum if they do not get to take it home with them. People in the world today take the same approach when it comes to the many blessings God has given us. God likely looks down upon us, wondering why we are so dissatisfied, why we are ungrateful, and why we act as if we know better than He does. Rather than questioning everything God does, we need to realize that everything God does is perfect. What if we devoted more time to worship than we spend making requests?

Keeping Our Eyes on Him

> *"Glory in his holy name; let the hearts of those who seek the Lord rejoice. Look to the LORD and his strength; seek his face always" (Ps. 105:3-4 NIV).*

Without doubt, there will be times in life when we question God's plan for our lives. We may experience moments when we wonder if God hears our cries for help. Yet, even in the situations that may cause us to question our faith, we need to follow the example of the psalmist David who said, "I keep my eyes always on the LORD. With him at my right hand, I will not be shaken" (Ps. 16:8 NIV). We must keep our eyes on Jesus Christ, for He is the only One who can help us through the darkest days and the vilest valleys of life.

Still, many people have a tendency to look to other people. Whether it is because they can physically see these individuals, or because they feel God is not listening to their prayers, some people go to great lengths to seek out other imperfect humans like themselves for help in times of trouble. Although they may be able to offer a few encouraging words or a supportive embrace, how can we expect someone else who is struggling through his or her own difficulties in life to singlehandedly bring us through a trial? Why should we even hint at the notion that another person could bring about restoration, healing, or redemption? In reality, people may often disappoint us and let us down. The only One on whom we can truly rely is the living Son of God. We cannot look to anyone else for guidance and direction in our lives. Jesus Christ is the only real source of eternal healing and lasting hope.

Instead of focusing our eyes on individuals who may or may

not have our best interest at heart, Hebrews 12:2 says we should keep our eyes on Jesus Christ. He is not only our Lord and Savior, but the book of Hebrews tells us He is the One who established our faith. He is the reason we have faith. He gives us the ability to run this race called life. Without His mercy and grace, as well as His protection, we could do nothing, and we would be nothing. When we look to Him for direction, then we will know we are running down the right road instead of some treacherous, off-road path, which will lead to our demise.

God's Word says we should not let anything hinder us from running this race, "since we are surrounded by such a great cloud of witnesses" (Heb. 12:1 NIV). The host of Heaven is looking down, observing our lives on this earth. As we travel down the road of life, people will also be observing us as Christians, looking to see how we react in certain situations. They will be watching to see if we pray and trust God, or if we become extremely angry when something does not go the way we expect. We cannot allow the discouraging moments in life to steal our joy. Most importantly, we cannot afford to allow these times to deteriorate our testimony as Christians. We must lay aside all of the burdens in life, trusting God to meet our every need. He will be with us through every battle we encounter, helping us emerge victorious, if we put our trust completely in Him.

Ultimately, Jesus knows more about enduring hardships than we do. Hebrews 12:2-3 (NIV) says, "For the joy set before him he endured the cross, scorning its shame, and sat down at the right hand of the throne of God. Consider him who endured such opposition from sinners, so that you will not grow weary and lose heart." Jesus hung on a cross for the forgiveness of our sins. If He could endure such agony, then why should we complain about our tiny little inconveniences? We should be ashamed at some of the trivial things about which we concern ourselves, considering the enormity of the sacrifice Jesus made for us. While there are significant troubles we must all face, we do not have to be alarmed, for Jesus will help us. He is sitting at the right hand of God interceding on our behalf (Rom. 8:34). The One who gave His life for us rose again on the third day, and He is now praying for us, making intercession for us, asking the Father to come to our aid.

Even so, some people fail to realize this significant fact. Rather than looking to Jesus for help, they have the false perception they can handle every problem all on their own. What's more, they may feel they can handle the situation even better than God can. Yet, our feeble human intervention will regularly lead to a roadblock on the road of life. Nee said, "We have to learn through bitter experience that we cannot *help* God, but we have the full power to *hinder* Him."[3] Consider a construction site where someone is standing in front of a bulldozer in order to *help* his or her fellow worker move some debris. Their behavior would only serve to halt all operations, due to the fact the machinery operator could not proceed with them standing in the way. In the same manner, we cannot stand between God and His will for us. We have to come to the absolute realization that God is in control. He knows best in every situation. We must allow Him to take the lead, never hindering His master plan for our lives.

Nevertheless, some people determine to put themselves first. They think they know best, so they remain laser-focused on what *they* want. Their focus is not on the Lord, but it is on living the best life they possibly can achieve. Instead of loving Jesus Christ, the Savior of the world, they primarily love themselves. Large numbers of preachers and teachers endorse this self-love doctrine from countless platforms at churches around the world. Many popular pastors promote the need to boost one's self-esteem as a central theme. Yet, the Bible says, "'Those who love their life in this world will lose it. Those who care nothing for their life in this world will keep it for eternity'" (John 12:25). Eternal life is only for individuals who do not favor their life over serving the Lord.

The apostle Paul said, "I have been crucified with Christ and I no longer live, but Christ lives in me. The life I now live in the body, I live by faith in the Son of God, who loved me and gave himself for me" (Gal. 2:20 NIV). Paul understood the fact that his life was not his own. He knew living his life for Christ should always be at the forefront of his existence. He cast aside his personal desires. Paul did not seek to serve himself; he longed to serve God. He wrote, "Those who belong to Christ Jesus have crucified the flesh with its passions and desires" (Gal. 5:24 NIV). His focus was not on his own earthly desires, but on God's will for his life. He kept his eyes on Jesus, living a life that was pleasing to our Heavenly Father.

The perspective of true worship gives God first place in our lives, not just a place.

We need to have the same perspective as Paul, fully realizing our purpose on this earth is not to fulfill our own desires, but to fulfill God's master plan for our lives. What we want to say, where we want to go, and what we want to do is irrelevant and inconsequential. The perspective of true worship gives God first place in our lives, not just a place. The erroneous pursuit of our own interests will not only prevent us from receiving all of the wonderful promises of God, but it could ultimately lead to disappointment or disaster. We cannot be like a child who disobeys their parents by swimming in dangerous rip current conditions, unaware of the risks involved. Instead, we need to be obedient to our Heavenly Father, trusting Him to guide us through life, recognizing the fact that He knows best in every situation. God has known us since before we were born (Isa. 49:1). He created us in His image (Gen. 1:27). He has numbered the hairs on our heads (Matt. 10:30). We are special in His sight. God loves us unconditionally. In His great love, He has mapped out every aspect of our lives for all eternity. God's plan does not entail living for ourselves, but living for God alone. He created us to worship Him.

Just as the shepherds and the Wise Men gave adoration to Jesus Christ, we must continually give God the glory He deserves. God is worthy of our praise. He is not a divine being in a faraway place. He is the God we can know on a personal level. He is "God with us" (Matt. 1:23). He desires fellowship with us. Worship is not an activity reserved for a certain place or time; it is the primary reason for our existence. Our daily mission in life should be to come before the Lord with a surrendered heart, glorifying Him because He is worthy of our praise. Whether we are worshiping at church, fulfilling our duties at work, or studying at school, we should always bring Him glory in everything we do. The privilege of communing with our Creator is one we should never take for granted. The God who created the heavens and the earth wants to hear from us. He is looking for those who will worship Him in spirit and in truth.

As we worship Him sincerely, the Spirit of the living God will fill our hearts and minds. As we become more completely devoted to the Lord, there will be little room in our hearts and minds for worldly pleasures. When we worship God wholeheartedly, loving Him with all of our hearts, our minds, and our souls, then we will be able to echo the words of Paul: "I have been crucified with Christ and I no longer live, but Christ lives in me. The life I now live in the body, I live by faith in the Son of God, who loved me and gave himself for me" (Gal. 2:20 NIV). In order to please God, we must take ourselves out of the picture. Our bodies are a temple of the Holy Spirit, not a house of worldly pleasure. God gave us the gift of life so we could live for Him. A worshipful life begins with surrendering our own will and putting Christ first in everything we do.

When we live a life of worship, then we will experience the mighty presence of God in our lives. Just as King Jehoshaphat experienced a divine miracle on the battlefield, we will also see the ways God moves when we place God at the center of our lives. Contrary to the individuals who believe the world revolves around them, a better point of view would be the perspective that the entire universe revolves around God. The Spirit of God is everywhere. God spoke the whole universe into existence. In His infinite wisdom and compassion, He also spoke you and me into existence. He wants to dwell within each one of us, for that is why He created us in His image. He created us to fellowship with Him forevermore.

God created us for worship. Although society attempts to prove otherwise, this world is not a platform for entertainment, even within the church. God did not create us so we could become a household name; He created us to lift up the name above all names, Jesus Christ. The reason we are on this earth is to bring glory to our Creator. We are not on this earth to pursue happiness; we are on this earth to pursue God. Why should we look to anyone or anything else other than the One who created us?

> *We are not on this earth to pursue happiness; we are on this earth to pursue God.*

Only God can give us never-ending joy and lasting hope. God has given us everything. Our lives belong to Him. We should devote our lives to worshiping Him, not only for spiritual fulfillment, but for the divine truth of who He is. He is the true and living God. He alone is worthy of our praise. God is the One we should worship every day of our lives.

God is not searching for people who worship Him once a

week, as they find a small window of time in-between everything from pursuing career goals to visiting entertainment venues, or those who worship Him only when they have a critical personal need. Jesus said, "'But the time is coming—indeed it's here now—when true worshipers will worship the Father in spirit and in truth. The Father is looking for those who will worship him that way'" (John 4:23). God is looking for people who worship Him for who He is, not simply for what He does. God created us to have meaningful fellowship with Him. Our purpose in life is to worship Him in spirit and in truth, not to worship our churches, workplaces, families, or any other entity on earth. God is not looking for people who worship Him alongside other idols in their lives. God is looking for true worshipers. May God help each one of us to take our eyes off the things and circumstances of this world, placing our focus on the only One who deserves our praise. God alone is worthy. He deserves *all* of the glory. Let us dedicate our lives to being the kind of worshipers the Lord is seeking as we worship God in spirit and in truth!

> *God is looking for people who worship Him for who He is, not simply for what He does.*

I love You, Lord.
I worship You.
I love You, Lord.
There is none like You.
My strength, my shield,
Forever be.
I love You, Lord.
You are Lord to me.

—*Jennifer Joy Campbell*

Acknowledgements

"Because your love is better than life, my lips will glorify you. I will praise you as long as I live, and in your name I will lift up my hands" (Ps. 63:3-4 NIV).

When I published my first book in June 2019, I had already begun the process of writing this book that you now hold in your hands. For more than a year, I have diligently sought the Lord as I have written the words on these pages. Yet, I could not have even written one word if it was not for the leading of the Holy Spirit. Without God's wisdom and guidance, I could not have completed this manuscript.

While my Heavenly Father is the One who made this book possible, I must also take a moment to thank my earthly father for his valuable contributions to my book. My dad, Ken Campbell, is such a blessing to me in a multitude of ways. I thank God for the blessing of a father who loves me unconditionally. He always supports me and encourages me in everything I do. He is a shining example of God's amazing love. My dad patiently listened to my thoughts and ideas along the way, often giving me godly counsel when it came to spiritual and theological topics. Additionally, he selflessly gave of his time to help critique and proofread the final draft. His careful consideration to the writing of such a thought-provoking foreword is truly an example of not only the love my dad has for me, but also the love he has for our Heavenly Father. My dad understands what it means to be a true worshiper, and he wholeheartedly gives all of the glory to God.

Additionally, I want to express my sincerest appreciation to the dear friends who wrote such gracious endorsements for this book. Thank you for placing the focus on worshiping God in spirit and in truth. Your heartfelt expressions exemplify the sentiments found in Proverbs 16:24: "Kind words are like honey—sweet to the soul and healthy for the body."

Although publishing my second book seems like a monumental accomplishment, this milestone holds no value on its own. Like the apostle Paul, I would say, "Everything else is worthless when compared with the infinite value of knowing Christ Jesus my Lord" (Phil. 3:8). My personal relationship with Jesus Christ is what gives my life meaning. He is the One who inspires me to keep pressing on. He is the reason I am alive today.

My aim in life is to serve the Lord in all I do. No matter what other people do or say, I have my feet planted firmly on the solid Rock, Jesus Christ. I will praise Him for all eternity, for He is great and greatly to be praised. My desire is to be the kind of true worshiper God is seeking. Therefore, I will never cease worshiping Him in spirit and in truth!

Notes

Foreword

1. Ken Campbell, "Preach the Word," 1986.

Introduction

1. Terry MacAlmon, "This Is the Time," track 1 on *Live Worship From the World Prayer Center*, TMMI Music, 2000.

Chapter One: Created for Worship

1. *Merriam-Webster.com Dictionary*, s.v. "worship," https://www.merriam-webster.com/dictionary/worship.
2. Ibid.
3. Ken Campbell, "Hope in Christ," Christ Will Return Ministries, http://www.christwillreturn.org/hopein christ.htm.
4. Lael Weinberger, "Evolution in American Education and the Demise of Its Public School System," Answers in Genesis, https://www.answersingenesis.org/public-school/evolution-in-us-education-and-demise-of-its-public-school-system.
5. Warren Wiersbe, *The Bible Exposition Commentary: New Testament*, vol. 1 (Colorado Springs, CO: David C. Cook, 1989), 518.

6.   A.W. Tozer, "The Purpose of Man," in *The Essential Tozer Collection*, 3-in-1 ed., comp. and ed. James L. Snyder (Minneapolis, MN: Bethany House, 2017), 46.

Chapter Two: Adore Him

1.   Warren Wiersbe, *From Worry to Worship: Studies in Habakkuk* (Lincoln, NE: Back to the Bible, 1983), 90.
2.   Flavius Josephus, "Antiquities of the Jews," in *The Complete Works of Flavius Josephus*, trans. William Whiston, (Grand Rapids, MI: Kregel, 1973), 92.
3.   Ibid.

Chapter Three: The Heart of Worship

1.   A.W. Tozer, *Tozer on Worship and Entertainment*, comp. James L. Snyder (Chicago, IL: WingSpread, 1997), 42.
2.   A.W. Tozer, "The Crucified Life," in *The Essential Tozer Collection*, 3-in-1 ed., comp. and ed. James L. Snyder (Minneapolis, MN: Bethany House, 2017), 204.

Chapter Four: The God We Know

1.   Martin Luther, *Luther's Works: The American Edition*, ed. Jaroslav Pelikan (St. Louis, MO: Concordia Publishing House, 1958), 1:185.
2.   Warren Wiersbe, *Real Worship: Playground, Battleground, or Holy Ground?* (Grand Rapids, MI: Baker Books, 2000), 59.

Chapter Five: Worship Not Entertainment

1. Jennifer Campbell, *When You're in the Sunset, There's Sunshine Awaiting You* (McAlpin, FL: Jennifer Joy Campbell, 2019), 247.
2. Ken Campbell, "Preaching or Foolishness," Christ Will Return Ministries, http://www.christwillreturn.org/preachingorfoolishness.htm.

Chapter Six: The Power of Praise

1. Jennifer Campbell, "Thank You, Lord," 2015, http://www.cwrmusic.org.
2. Watchman Nee, *Worship God* (New York, NY: Christian Fellowship Publishers, 1990), 43.

Chapter Seven: Worship Replaces Worry

1. Carol Cymbala and Ann Spangler, *He's Been Faithful: Trusting God to Do What Only He Can Do* (Grand Rapids, MI: Zondervan, 2001), 73.

Chapter Eight: A Life of Worship

1. MacAlmon, "This Is the Time."
2. Jim Cymbala, "A Year of Praise" (sermon, Brooklyn Tabernacle, Brooklyn, NY, December 31, 2019).
3. Ken Campbell, "Grace, So Amazing," 2017.
4. Ibid.

Chapter Nine: God Deserves the Glory

1. Tozer, "The Crucified Life," 121.
2. Leonard Ravenhill, *Why Revival Tarries* (Minneapolis, MN: Bethany Fellowship, 1959), 49.
3. Jennifer Campbell, "Jesus Gave His Life for Love," 2013, http://www.cwrmusic.org.
4. Wiersbe, *The Bible Exposition Commentary: New Testament*, 248.
5. Ken Campbell, "God Is Love," Christ Will Return Ministries, http://www.christwillreturn.org/godislove.htm.

Chapter Ten: Worship in Heaven

1. Tozer, "The Purpose of Man," 98.
2. Ravenhill, *Why Revival Tarries*, 35.
3. Fanny J. Crosby and W.H. Doane, "Rescue the Perishing," in *Melodies of Praise* (Springfield, MO: Gospel Publishing House, 1957), 177.
4. Ibid.
5. Ibid.

Chapter Eleven: The Spirit of the Living God

1. Tozer, "The Purpose of Man," 79.
2. "Abortion Information," National Right to Life, https://www.nrlc.org/abortion.
3. Cymbala, "A Year of Praise."
4. Ken Campbell, "What Can I Give to the King?," 2005.

Chapter Twelve: God Seeks True Worshipers

1. Ravenhill, *Why Revival Tarries*, 99.
2. Ken Campbell, "He Gave His All," 2005.
3. Nee, *Worship God*, 84.

Acknowledgements

1. Jennifer Campbell, "I Worship You," 2020.

About the Author

*J*ennifer Joy Campbell was born and raised in the Sunshine State of Florida, where she and her father, Ken, share a home on their small family farm with their orange and white tabby cat, Morris. She also enjoys spending time with her Grandma Lucille.

Jennifer is a talented author, speaker, and web designer. On June 27, 2019, she published her first book, an inspirational autobiography titled, *When You're in the Sunset, There's Sunshine Awaiting You.* She is host of the *Be Encouraged* webcast, viewed each week by thousands of people representing all parts of the globe.

Jennifer is a graduate of Florida Gateway College (Lake City, Florida), the University of Florida (Gainesville, Florida), and Nova Southeastern University (Fort Lauderdale, Florida). She completed her Master of Science degree in English education with a 4.0 GPA. Following her dad's example, she is now in her fifteenth year of teaching. She currently teaches for Suwannee Virtual School and serves as an adjunct English professor for Toccoa Falls College.

Her dad, Ken, served as a high school and college mathematics instructor, having thirty-five years' experience in the field of education. In the summer of 2019, he retired from public education to devote more time to the ministry.

In addition to being educators, this father-daughter team enjoys cooking and baking. They are always experimenting with new creations in the kitchen, both sweet and savory, from fresh-baked cookies and cakes to homemade pasta and artisan bread.

Jennifer and her dad are involved in a worldwide missionary

outreach, Christ Will Return Ministries. The focus of this ministry is to call attention to the return of Jesus Christ, to proclaim the Gospel to those who are lost, and to encourage believers to share the love of Christ boldly.

Ken and Jennifer are both gifted songwriters and accomplished pianists. They produce their recordings in-house using a large number of acoustic instruments as well as sampled orchestral notes from the Vienna Symphonic Library.

Jennifer and her dad have also written many Gospel tracts, a number of which have been translated into approximately twenty languages. They frequently travel to various parts of the world to share the Gospel and sing of His love. They consider it a blessing to have visited more than fifty-five countries and territories around the world. God has been with them each step of the way.

Ken and Jennifer make their Gospel articles, Jennifer's *Be Encouraged* webcast, and a number of their songs freely available online for the widest possible distribution worldwide at www.christwillreturn.org. For one day soon, Christ will return.

Contact Jennifer:

Christ Will Return Ministries
Website: www.christwillreturn.org
Email: jennifer@christwillreturn.org

Free Music Download

Visit **www.cwrmusic.org** for a free MP3 download of Jennifer's song titled, "Thank You, Lord." May God use this song to encourage you today!

Jennifer's Inspirational Autobiography

When You're in the Sunset,
There's Sunshine Awaiting You

*J*ennifer Campbell endured the very first trial of her life when she was born without a heartbeat. When she was sixteen years old, her life was in jeopardy once again. Through her experiences, she was inspired to write a song titled, "There's Sunshine Awaiting You." Years later, God used this song to minister to Jennifer's own heart during a very dark season of her life. Having overcome many difficulties, her greatest desire is to share the message of hope.

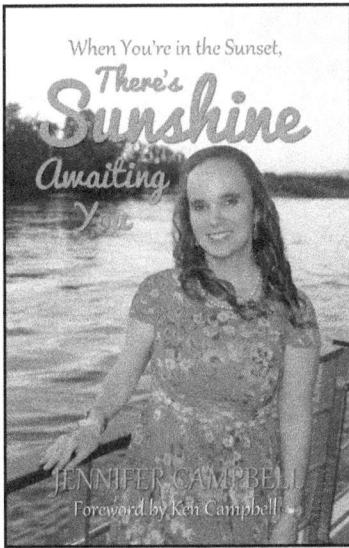

Jennifer knows firsthand that it is in the sunsets of life where we can find true restoration, true peace, and true comfort in the knowledge that Jesus Christ, the One who loves us more than we could ever imagine, will never leave us nor forsake us. When we put our trust in His master plan for our lives, we will have hope even in the most discouraging situations. No matter what you are facing today, be encouraged. For even in the sunset, there is sunshine awaiting you.

Read a free chapter at www.jennifercampbell.net/sunshine.

Available on Amazon.
ISBN: 978-0-9600359-1-5 (softcover)
ISBN: 978-0-9600359-0-8 (eBook)

www.ingramcontent.com/pod-product-compliance
Lightning Source LLC
Chambersburg PA
CBHW030103070426
42448CB00037B/910